FROM BASIC TO BAGHDAD

FROM BASIC TO BAGHDAD

JB HOGAN

A Soldier Writes Home

BRAVE IDEAS

Dover, DE

From Basic to Baghdad: A Soldier Writes Home
by JB Hogan
Published by Brave Ideas, PO Box 333, Cheswold, DE 19936
www.frombasictobaghdad.com

Interior illustrations by Luke Siler.
Cover and interior design by Pneuma Books, LLC
Visit www.pneumabooks.com for more information.

Library of Congress Cataloging-In-Publication Data

Hogan, J. B.
　From basic to Baghdad : a soldier writes home / JB Hogan.
　　p. cm.
　Includes bibliographical references and index.
　ISBN-13: 978-1-892427-16-8 (hardback : alk. paper)
　ISBN-10: 1-892427-16-8
　　1. Iraq War, 2003--Personal narratives, American. 2. Soldiers--United States--Correspondence.　I. Title.

　DS79.76.H65 2005
　956.7044'373--dc22

LCCN: 2005011913

10　09　08　07　06　05　　　　　　6　5　4　3　2　1

To everyone who signed up for the college money

TABLE OF CONTENTS

PUBLISHER'S PREFACE

It was spring 2001. Our oldest son, JB, had been depressed and angry during the long winter months and was just starting to show signs of being ready to tackle life again. Academically gifted and highly motivated during his younger years, JB had graduated early and received his diploma from our homeschool association. He spent a semester at Grove City College near Pittsburgh where the dark and dreary weather adversely affected him. We brought him home and he began working part-time and taking classes at University of Delaware.

In May, JB unexpectedly quit his job. Although he was still somewhat moody, we felt it was important for him to either go back to school full-time or get a full-time job. His dream of being a writer, we said, wouldn't support him initially. We suggested he either finish his education or commit to the workforce, all the while stockpiling experiences to use in his writing. We knew him well enough to know that he would do better in a structured environment. He was not easy to live with and his brooding angst was taking a toll on all of us, especially our younger son, Tyler.

June arrived, and Bob, Tyler, and I were at a conference in North Carolina where I was speaking on homeschooling topics. JB phoned. He casually announced that a Marine recruiter had called him and suggested he come in to talk. JB asked what we thought about him enlisting. Bob and I said that we'd pray about it, while secretly we were all but doing handstands.

JB didn't like the Marine recruiter. He said that he was "being fed a line." So, he decided to visit each of the Armed Forces represented in the building to see who would offer him the best deal. Turned out the army was paying big bucks for buck privates. JB agreed to give the United States Army four years of his life, harboring visions of paying off his motorcycle and his credit card with plenty leftover for spending and investments. Although he received a perfect score on the entrance exam, he was told that there were only openings for "cooks, drivers, or infantry." JB chose infantry, with the goal of becoming a Ranger.

When JB told us that he'd actually enlisted, we were alternately appalled and pleased. On the one hand, we think the military is an honorable and important institution. Bob's dad retired from the army and my dad served in the navy during WWII. We believed the discipline and structure would be great for our son. On the other hand, the JB we knew balked at taking orders, never had any interest in guns, and preferred reading to all other activities. Somehow, this did not seem like the perfect fit!

Nevertheless, he enlisted on a Monday and, having agreed to an "early ship" because of the extra bonus it provided, left for boot camp at Fort Benning, Georgia, that Thursday.

I knew that he would need moral support and prayer, so I began to disseminate his letters to a few family and friends, encouraging them to write back. JB's love of writing became his lifeline home. Although all of his letters from basic were handwritten, I typed each one and sent them out by email. Not only was this more efficient than photocopying his letters, very few people would be willing to decipher his handwriting.

In these email broadcasts I would occasionally insert little comments that I jokingly called "Editor's Notes" (not realizing that much later they really would be editor's notes!) to clarify something here and there. Mostly, I was just having fun.

Then life turned solemn. Right before JB was due to graduate from basic and advanced infantry training, 9/11 changed everything. Although he had already showed great signs of growth physically, emotionally, and spiritually, 9/11 caused JB to take the army seriously. Thus began a new chapter in his life.

After his graduation, he was slated for Airborne School. There he sustained two stress fractures in his final run. This ended his shot at Ranger School. Instead, he was assigned to the Third Infantry Division in Fort Benning.

From there, to his first deployment to Kuwait, to the events leading up to the Third Infantry's assault on Baghdad, we kept sending updates and prayer requests on JB's behalf. More and more people requested to be on our mailing list, and JB received more and more mail from perfect strangers. He absolutely loved this, and it helped to keep his morale up, knowing that folks all over cared for him and were praying for him. It became my personal mission to be his cheerleader/communications director/prayer warrior.

By this time, many people had suggested that his trail of letters and emails should be compiled into a book. I jokingly said if I did, I'd call it "Dave Barry Joins the Army" because JB's humor often reminded me of the columnist. But because Bob and I own a small independent publishing company, the idea grew on us. After prayer and consideration, we agreed to take the innumerable pieces of correspondence that we'd saved haphazardly in files, boxes, inboxes, and on a variety of random surfaces and try to organize it.

Fortunately, we knew a wonderful young lady named Hannah Eagleson, a recent graduate of St. John's College, who was willing to attempt this task. She did a great job and we were then able to hand off the editing and creative design to the fine folks at Pneuma Books. The team there latched on to the idea and became personally invested in making this book the best book it could be.

Looking back, I can only marvel at God's grace and goodness in JB's life. From a stubborn, angry teen with the requisite long hair, God drew JB to Himself and began a new work in his heart. I think it all boils down to this: God has a purpose for everyone's life and He uses His people in remarkable ways. As you read about JB's purpose during these past dramatic years, we hope you will join us in giving God the glory, and honor, and praise.

— Maggie Hogan, Publisher,
aka cheerleader/prayer warrior/mom/
communications director

A NOTE FROM THE AUTHOR

When I started writing these letters, I did not intend for them to be compiled or published. All I wanted to do was to share my experiences in basic training with my parents. Little did I know that my mother was taking my handwritten letters and typing them up on her computer, editing and spell checking them, and sending them out to extended family, friends, business contacts, strangers she met in the store, and so forth.

It wasn't until a few months into basic training that I found out what was happening with my epistles. I started receiving packages and notes from tons of people, many of whom were completely unknown to me. I questioned my mother at the next opportunity.

Me: So, who's the Farklesmatter family? Why are they sending me birthday cards?

Mom: I'm not sure. They probably get your letters forwarded to them from someone on the mailing list.

Me: What mailing list?

Mom: The mailing list for your newsletter.

Me: Newsletter?

Apparently, my deepest personal issues that I'd intended to reveal only to my parents had become dinner table conversation for utter strangers around the United States. [Editor's Note: Well, the world, actually.] This caused me to make minor changes in content and style in my letters home, but it also gave me a new kind of freedom. I had a captive audience and I could practice being as funny, dramatic, or thought provoking as I wanted to be.

So this collection began. At first it was merely an 80-page stack of letters detailing my experiences in basic training: from trying desperately to get out, to the 9/11 attacks, and then to my newfound commitment to completing my army training. But that was it — until we deployed to Kuwait. Then I remembered my audience from basic training and decided if they thought *that* was funny they would surely get a kick out of the hoops we were jumping through out in the desert. Shortly after our Kuwait deployment we were sent off to fight a war in Iraq. Once again I did my best to keep my extended fan base informed, and my mother diligently compiled my correspondence. When I finally returned from the war, I saw just how much I had actually produced and decided there was the potential for a book.

I filled in the gaps from the war with the help of the journal I kept and a few pictures gathered from various friends and fellow soldiers. The final touch came in the form of some wonderful cartoons done by my best friend, Luke Siler, which make the perfect addition.

I hope you enjoy reading it half as much as I've enjoyed writing it.

✐ P.S. Keep an eye out for the paper clip icons at the beginning of letters and emails. This is an indication that there is a corresponding number of cartoons and/or pictures that accompany the letter or email.

From now on, Dover's water supply will be chlorinated

By JOYCE MULLINS
Staff Writer

For many years the City of Dover has said it has the chlorinated water that Mother Earth's deep aquifers can provide.

Not everyone agreed that Dover water was the best tasting. Some residents in certain parts of the city say the water has the odor of rotten eggs, which they say affects the taste.

Odd odors notwithstanding, Dover's water has fared well in public perception and has even taken top awards in water quality and taste competitions with other municipalities. And one of its claims to fame was that its pristine qualities have been unadulterated by chlorine.

Sometime before the year is out, that's changing.

To make sure that Dover's water supply remains safe and clean for generations to come, the city is beginning continuous chlorination this year.

According to state Division of Public Health Office of Drinking Water, Public Water Supply Supervision Program Manager Anita Beckel, "Chlorination will improve the aesthetic quality of the water in the areas that have taste and odor complaints from hydrogen sulfide the rotten egg odor."

The state routinely runs tests on the city's water supply. The Total Coliform Rule requires water systems to meet stricter limits for coliform bacteria. Finding coliform bacteria in the water can be an indication of disease-causing bacteria. When that happens, follow-up testing is done.

If the strict limit is exceeded, the water supplier — in this case, the City of Dover — is put on public notice, meaning the public is told through newspapers, radio and television broadcasts.

Growth is one factor in the decision to begin continuous chlorination.

Beckel, in the Division's Public Water Supply Supervision section, said, "I think they had operated the system very carefully for years and had been able to go without chlorination and it was a great job. It was great management not to have to do continuous chlorination for this long."

BASIC TRAINING

Dear Mom — Help!

📎 Letter from JB dated June 18, 2001

Dear Everybody (and then some),

Hello. You have probably all forgotten me by now. This is JB. Remember? The tall guy! No...that's Luke you are thinking of. Anyway, for those of you who do not remember, I joined the army a couple of days ago.

Yeah, all that free food and revelry at my house? That was me, leaving. But don't worry, there's probably all kinds of interesting stuff happening to you guys and I'm sure I'd love to hear all about it. Of course, that means you'll have to write me, you lazy bums.

This letter has assumed an astonishingly irritated tone. My apologies. In the words of Inigo Montoya, "Let me 'splain. No, is too long; let me sum up..." [Editor's Note: this obscure reference is from one of JB's favorite movies, one even I approve of — *The Princess Bride*.]

(*Scene Fades*)

(*A Cafeteria*)

STAGE DIRECTIONS: Assorted generic humans scattered about. Enter our hero looking dashing and sexy despite being up since four and unshowered because his official wake up call consisted of "Err...we forgot your room. Uh...sorry...If you hurry you can catch the bus..."

SERGEANT WHATEVER: "All of you! I'm gonna call your assignment and you guys get up and...and leave!" (This is actually a summary, because this simple concept took the sergeant about five minutes before everyone got it. Interesting side note: the women demonstrated a much higher "explanation of concept to grasp of subject matter" ratio. This doesn't play into my theories at all ... oh no!)

Anyway, the various branches all filtered out to their assignments except! Guess who? Us! Us poor Benning guys. We huddled in the back like stoats [Editor's Note: A stoat is similar to a weasel. JB reads too much.] confronted with a bulldozer and pretended that we weren't worried that there were no tickets or orders or even eye contact emanating from Sergeant What's-Her-Face toward us. She leaves. (A lot of time seemed to be packed into about 20 seconds here...) She pops her head back into the room.

"You guys Benning?" (Sentence structure and logical equivalence are not required to be a sergeant. In a strategic career move, I decided not to say anything.)

"Yes."

"Well, you guys are all screwed up. Go find out what's wrong."

Gotta love the military. The chief transportation officer in the building has given us peons the privilege — nay! honor! — of finding out what has happened to our transportation! We formulated an action plan that started with us standing up and then consisted of us wandering around. Ah! The innovation that a human mind is capable of in strange situations.

So, it turns out (We have fast forwarded a bit here. It's about the equivalent of pressing stop, pressing fast forward, and then eating an entire block of Velveeta before pressing play) that there is like a storm or tornado or a giant bat or something over Charlotte. [Editor's Note: I presume he's referring to Charlotte, North Carolina, airspace, not an enlistee by the same name.]

I voted we brave it out because in terms of overall nastiness, dying in a plane attacked by a giant bat is equal to basic training but quicker. But one thing that is required of a sergeant is the kind of mindset that makes one prefer consuming feta cheese through one's nostrils rather than listening to the applicants who are directly affected by the decision being made.

So they tell us to sit. "Be all you can be" is not the army's motto. "Go and have a seat" is.

Press fast forward. Have another block of Velveeta. They finally decide that they are gonna get somebody to drive us back to the hotel. Apparently they couldn't decide between that and having us sleep on the tables in the cafeteria. I love the army! They always consider all their options.

So we get driven back to the hotel. We discovered that the military station was closed! No rules! So we each devised a personal plan of action. Mine involved *Seinfeld*. So anyway, I watched TV then went to sleep. Then we got up, got on a bus, then on an airplane, then on another airplane, then on a bus, then here — the most boring place on Earth.

Apparently the seven of us, because we were late, are generating a massive SEP field. For those of you who haven't broadened your horizons by reading Douglas Adams, and for Luke who has but has surely forgotten, an SEP is "somebody else's problem." It makes us effectively invisible.

Nobody has any clue what to do with us or where to put us. We missed processing so we have to wait until the 25th to get started on everything. *Right now our job is this: Nothing! Plus, since we have only civilian clothes, we go to the front of the meal line. No lie, if you are at the end of the line, you wait over two hours to get food.

There is a disadvantage to this though. To find out what it is, re-read the sentence with asterisk in front. Very boring. So boring I'm writing home, even though — and make careful note of this — absolutely nothing noteworthy has happened yet!

So, it's pretty impressive that I've managed to write however many pages I've written so far. [Editor's Note: It's hard to ascertain how many pages he did write since the pages were all marked with random numbers.]

Interesting side note: you can't write back to me yet. I have no address since we haven't processed yet. So enjoy this one — it's a freebie. The next one you must reply to or... else. You know. We haven't been trained on threats. Yet.

Anyway, I've pretty much caught ya'll up to date, so I'm gonna stop for a bit. I can't send this yet because I don't know where the mail goes. If anything interesting happens, I'll add it. But in case I don't, here is an ending. I miss everybody and I'll see you eventually, unless I die. Or you die. Either one.

~JB

Letter from JB dated June 25, 2001

Dear Everybody,

So we just shipped out. We are now at a halfway house. It has emphasized to what a great extent the army has crushed us: when we arrived here we were given individual wall lockers, and the men were near tears of joy. Back home if we had to fit our stuff in one of these, we'd have been dialing 800-1Bad-Dad in two seconds. But I love my locker. It may be absolutely small but it is relatively huge, and I still smile every time I gaze upon her gunmetal gray glory. Oh yeah!

Next day

I like it much better here. Some of the guys close to my bunk share a few interests: music, video games, and movies. Actually, for a little while I forgot where I was. Of course, when I remembered, it all came back pretty hard.

I miss all of you guys back home and from what it looks like I'll be seeing you again in November or so. Every now and again it strikes me that I will probably never live at home or in Dover again. I didn't want to grow up. I don't know what I was thinking! Gonna sign off. We missed mail call Monday so I hope to be reading letters tonight. Bye.

~JB

Letter from JB dated June 27, 2001

Hi Everyone,

I'm writing this letter in the middle of a huge commotion. We were told to rearrange our wall lockers and bunks so that they match those in bay 1. Since our bay had an organic, free-form pattern that "breathed" and gave space while remaining compact and able to house enough men, while the other was tight, rigid, and gave the appearance of conserving more space at the cost of making it a nightmare to get to your stuff, the drill sergeant leapt into action with standardization on his mind. Both bays must be army style! Like all army stuff: tight, rigid, and giving the appearance of efficiency.

Yesterday I was sick again. I finally broke down and decided to go to sick call. They gave me some pills that have really helped actually. So other than a nonstop drip and a headache, I'm okay.

I am so desperate for reading materials that I am reading *Yoga Philosophy* which is assuring me that with enough positive energy and spiritual thinking I can develop psychic powers and wander around in the Astral plane. While this is good for a laugh (especially since it is written in eastern instructional style — which means never bothering to prove your points), I'm really hungering for something that is intentionally humorous!

Next day

This morning we had a good 120 minutes of PT. I was burning! For one part we had to hold our arms out at shoulder height, palms up, for half an hour. Try doing that until your arms hurt, then rotate them around in tiny circles. Unbelievable!

I had a pair of boots stolen from me. It is very frustrating. I'm gonna have to pay for a new pair.

How long have I been gone? I'm really losing track of time. I guess it hasn't really been that long, especially for you guys back home. But it has been an eternity here. You guys are probably just starting to notice that JB never hangs out with you anymore. I still can't believe I joined up!

Just got back from mail call. Didn't get anything...don't feel bad, I know writing a letter is a huge time commitment. And hearing from home isn't that important: it's only the absolute highlight of any army day. No pressure.

Well, I'm about done with this general letter. It's time to reply personally to the people who wrote me. Just think! A personalized letter from JB. It could happen to you.

~JB

Hello Everyone,

We're finally shipping to BCT [Editor's Note: Ha!] on Thursday. I have mixed feelings about this. On one hand, I am ready to get things going and start the clock running toward the good stuff. On the other hand, I'm relatively comfortable here and I can handle it. BCT is going to be a lot rougher. But it's not like I have any choice. I signed that away a year ago. Well, okay, it was only a couple of weeks ago, but we're discussing things in emotional terms here; let's not ruin that with the facts.

They didn't make us do any PT today. That was great — my body really needs to heal. I've got a terrible headache and sinus congestion. I've taken some medicine, which helps a little, but I'm still in constant pain. I hope to be well by Thursday.

They let us go to the rec center for a few hours. I was happy. There were video games and ice cream! After that I checked out a bass and was able to jam for a while. It felt good to play. In one of the booths there was a drum kit, so next time I'll have to try to play with someone.

I have begun receiving the first of the letters from home.

Thank you so much. To those who write, I promise a personalized response (which will be worth a serious chunk of change when I'm famous) and to those who don't write, I promise only swift and painful revenge. So, you've got options.

I have decided that I'm definitely going to get out of these enlisted ranks as soon as possible. These people are just too stupid! I can almost feel my mental prowess being drained away as if there are mind vampires all about.

I know my writing has certainly suffered. I have tremendous difficulty thinking of anything funny to say. I fear that within a week my sense of humor will be dead. Please send me a whoopee cushion to bury it in.

So, now I'm on fire watch. Fire watch is yet another way the army has discovered to make life a little less pleasant for the smallest amount of effective return on time spent. Basically, for every hour of the night, three people must be awake. One of them must stand outside in uniform. He's the one that lost the coin toss. The two inside have the job to wander around listlessly and complain. That's something I'm good at.

Monday

Boy, Sunday was something to write about! For some reason they couldn't feed us here at the halfway house. So they bussed all of us back to the 30th AG. Now you have to understand that even though there is nothing to do here, at least we can do nothing inside. At the 30th AG we had to wait outside between meals. On metal bleachers. In full BDUs. People were passing out.

My headache is worse again today, and I think I have yesterday to thank for it. They also had us pick grass. Fortunately, I was in chapel [Editor's Note: Read that last phrase again!] during most of it, but some of the guys were picking individual strands of grass for hours. Individual. Strands. Of grass.

I'll keep writing as further events develop. Write!

~JB

Dear Home,

Well, quite a bit has happened since I last wrote, and virtually all of it needs complaining about. So let's get started!

July fourth had to be my absolute worst day yet. Forty of us were selected to go back to the 30th to eat. Naturally, they forgot about us, which wasn't so bad except we had to wait outside, and instead of being 30 minutes late, we didn't get back until after dinner! So what was everyone else doing? They went to the rec center for three hours and then got to picnic and watch fireworks! To make it up to us after we pointed out the inconsistency — they ignored us. Technically, being ignored is better than being noticed, but still...

We also mysteriously ran out of warm water that day, so the shower went from being the light at the end of the tunnel to the, uh, big nasty unpleasant thing...total analogy failure...

Today we were told to pack our gear because we are shipping out in the morning. But they weren't sure, so we had to move our stuff (90 lbs.) up and down three flights of stairs...twice.

So this brings you up to date — right to the very second that I'm writing.

So enough history, let's have some literature. I got more mail from people. The one from Luke was especially uplifting — I haven't laughed in a while. Please keep on writing.

I'm dropping the Ranger school. RIP is 19.5 hours a day, seven days a week. I just want to get out of the enlisted ranks as soon as possible.

But now it is Friday and we're finally shipping to BCT. After I'm there a little while I'll finally be able to start telling you what an average day is like. But wait! What's this? JB isn't shipping today! Of course everyone else is. JB is being held over. Why? Because back on the 30th some worthless lowlife stole his boots! So now I'm back at the halfway house. I'm stuck with a bunch of strangers and I have no clue what's going on. I am permanently separated from my previous group. My address will probably change — so I'll keep you posted. Keep writing to the current one for now.

I'm having very mixed feelings about BCT. I don't know if I can make it through or not. Part of me is glad I didn't ship. Part of me wants my contract voided so I can just go home. But I also want to make it and say I completed it. But guess what my reward for that is? Being owned by the army for four years.

I have met extremely few people here that I consider even worth knowing. And even out of those few it's not like I've clicked with anybody. Four years with no friends seems pretty bad.

So I think I'd like to fake my death. There is a life insurance policy with my name. I can finish BCT and then pretend to die during leave. I'm thinking I'll dig up a body and have it get in a fatal wreck. It'll have my dog tags around its neck. Between the life insurance and the fabulously popular novel I'll write, I'll be set for life. Sure beats four years of enlisted grade paychecks and base housing. It always feels good to have a plan. So if anyone can help me pull this off effectively, please let me know when I get back. It'll be fun.

So what's been going on up north? My estimation is that it's ten times as interesting and exciting up there, so that means I should be getting about ten times as much back as I send, okay? Make your letters worth the push-ups I have to do for them!

It's hot here. So naturally we wear long clothing, an undershirt, and boots with thick socks. Be prepared! For the wrong thing! Just as long as you are prepared for something! [Editors Note: I think JB was loudly declaring a twisted motto of some sort but one can never tell.]

Can't wait to get out!

(And I haven't even gotten in yet....)

~JB

Letter from JB dated July 7, 2001

Dear Everybody,

Well, it stinks big time that I didn't get to ship. Apparently it's even affected my loquacious ways; I never say something braindead like "stinks big time." Usually it's "stinks like Charybdis yawning," or something.

But I digress. Which is something which I excel at. But it is making it difficult for me to get to my point, which is this: although not shipping bites like a deranged pit bull, this current situation may not be as bad as I assumed.

For starters, we got to go to the rec center for three hours today. I was first in line to get a brand new bass and an amp that actually had volume. There was a drummer in the far room and we had been jamming for about ten minutes [Editor's Note: Presumably they came together in the same room to jam, at least one hopes.] when a guitarist overheard us and decided to join in. It was great. We must have played for two hours. I didn't quit until I couldn't play another note. I have a huge blood blister now.

I also got my hands on a real four string and played it until my fingers bled.

Then I had an Oreo milkshake and called home. You know, for a while I had forgotten I was in the army. So here's some news: I'm supposed to ship Monday.

Sunday

Well, I missed chapel today; I was disappointed by that. [Editor's Note: If you heard someone shouting yippee — it was me!] We had to be in BDUs to go and mine were filthy. I got to catch up on a little sleep though, which was nice.

Here's some good news: the guy who played drums with me is in this bay. That is a good start. If we ship out together, there is a good chance that we'll be able to play together at BCT. There are a few guys here who aren't so bad. Notice I haven't said "seem pretty cool" or anything like that. But, it is a start.

One guy has been taking Kung Fu for 10 years and he is teaching a few of us. We have mini sparring sessions at night. That is pretty fun. When I get to my station, I'm gonna start professional lessons.

Later

Well, it looks totally definite and final, conclusive even. We are shipping tomorrow. I got the boots free too! That was a major answer to prayer. [Editor's Note: Ditto!] Boots are around $70!

Oh, I am definitely shipping with the drummer guy but unfortunately I won't ship with any of the Kung Fu guys. It's soooo boring right now. For reasons both complicated and astoundingly dull, we won't eat until 8:00 P.M. Excuse me, 2000 hours. So we are waiting...forever...I almost wish something terrible would happen so I could write about it. Sigh.

Much later

Well I'm here at boot camp now. There's lots to tell, but we have no free time. I just need to get this out.

~JB

[Editor's Note: This letter was postmarked July 12th. It arrived along with a form letter from the U.S. Army that said JB was, indeed, officially in boot camp.]

✎ Letter from JB dated July 13, 2001

Dear Home,

I am stealing a moment here to write. I'm probably not supposed to, but I gotta lighten my load a bit. It is nuts here. We are busy 19 hours a day. I have never been so tired in my life as when I hit my bed.

I'm not very good at PT, but I'm still amazed at what I am able to do already. This morning we ran three miles before 0600. On the last half mile the guy behind me stumbled and hit my foot.

I fell out hard, but I was still able to get up and get back in the formation. I was proud of myself.

The run was horrible. Of course, they don't tell you how long you are going to run at the beginning — you just start running. After a while every lap seemed unbearable — it *had* to be the last one. But it never was.

We do so much stuff here. Only it's very little on paper. We have classes and we exercise. We clean our bunks and we get smoked. All the time. There's always one idiot who hurts the whole platoon.

I haven't gotten any mail in ages. I'm sure they are having trouble forwarding it since I got held over back then. I am very sad. I need news from home. I'll probably get stuff you write to the new address sooner than some of the old stuff.

I really don't want to do this anymore. It's not the basic though. I know I can make it and graduate. It's those four years after that have me terrified. I don't mesh well with these people here, and soon I will be stationed and living with them in foreign surroundings.

And as reclusive as I can get — even surrounded by great friends and family — I shudder to think what may happen there. I just want to come home now, work some boring job or something, and go to U of D in the fall.

However, I'm gonna stick it out for a few weeks. I don't want the DIS to think I'm trying to quit after the first few days. It's not the basic that I can't handle. What was I thinking? Well, I want to write more, but there's not time.

~JB

Dear Home,

So, it looks like we have time to write after all. I am just totally lost here. I don't know if this is where God wants me. I really feel I could come back home and do much better for myself in the civilian world. I'm aching — absolutely aching — with creative energy, stories, music, and all kinds of stuff. I think with a college degree I could make something of myself and not have to work for some company. And I *know* that the army is no place to be creative. (Pardon the disjointed thoughts — JB is ranting *and* experimenting with stream of consciousness writing...)

I just have to find out whether I can get general discharge not dishonorable. The dishonorable might haunt me later. It's frustrating how people look at paper and not the person. Of course, I'm not even sure I can get out. I'm gonna have to play it cool for a while and feel things out.

Sunday

Well, it is Sunday morning now and I am waiting for it to be chapel time. I am looking forward to that since I missed last week. The only downside to Sunday is that there is no mail. Not that they've given us any yet. I think I will risk the DI's wrath and ask about it.

We have a test today. We have to know the Infantryman's Creed, the chain of command, a motto or two, and a bunch of stuff about the rifle. I'm not concerned at all but one guy in the class is way far ADD (or just dumb), and I know we are gonna get smoked because of him.

We get smoked a lot. I am really sore and I have ugly bruises on my feet from these stupid boots. I have yet to receive my second pair — even though the DIs know about it. At least next week some of the good stuff starts. We begin shooting on Monday or Tuesday. Of course, that means chem suits and gas chamber on Saturday. Chaplain likened the chamber to hell: "there is smoke and fire, wailing and gnashing of teeth, and everybody wants out." But it's only for 60 seconds or so (although I've discovered that can be really long depending on what you're doing at the time).

I've decided to try to stick it out for at least the first part of August. That way I can show that I'm not just afraid of boot camp. If I can make it through the hard parts at the beginning maybe they will take me seriously when I say I need to get out. Also, if I get out in August I can still go to U of D in the fall. I figure I'll wait tables for a few hours a night to pay bills.

Wow, it's amazing all the things that I have given up: Velveeta, video games, deodorant, sleep, fun, books, all kinds of stuff. And you know, I can really do fine without most of that stuff. Although when I get home I'm gonna assault the library. [Editor's Note: I believe that is a figure of speech.]

In about 20 minutes we are starting another three-mile run. I'm not really looking forward to it. Afterwards we'll probably clean up and go to bed. I think I'll have fire watch so I'll probably write some more then if I can.

Chapel was okay. We have a female chaplain and I don't like her as much. Her message seems to be: The Bible says never give up, so keep pushing, men. And that's good — applying the Bible to the army lifestyle, but it's not very deep. The other guy was good at talking about Christian concepts but didn't always bring it to the practical level. Somewhere in between lies a good sermon. I want to get back to Grace Presbyterian. Church. I miss it there.

Monday

Wow, it is only lunchtime and I am so unbelievably beat. First thing in the morning we did push-ups and sit-ups until muscle failure. Then we did more by having a partner pull you up. Then we ate. After that we marched 1.5 miles to the obstacle course. That was really harsh. We had to run, jump, climb ropes, back crawl under barbed wire, and then bear crawl and crab walk half a football field. If you finished any event you had to run in place waiting for the rest of your group. I was so dead afterwards. Only, instead of marching to lunch like everyone else, our drill sergeants surprised us by "letting" us run it again. Then I was dead. However, as a reward (unless we screw up, which we probably will) we get phone time, 10 – 15 minutes or so this weekend.

I'm starting to have second thoughts about my second thoughts. Maybe I should stick it out. It would feel really great to graduate. Of course, there are all those years after to think about...I dunno. Pray for some serious guidance here. I've been asking God what I should do, but He's not telling right now. So help me keep bugging Him.

Later

Well, never mind about the phone time this weekend. This platoon is totally screwed up. I hate these losers. Some moron complained about a simple command from the DI and refused to work. Now, not only did we lose phone privileges, but we are not allowed in the bay all day. In between stuff we have to stay outside, standing at attention. This place...I'm so tired of being punished for stuff I had nothing to do with — or worse yet, for orders I never heard. Both of our stupid DIs tend to give commands to the entire bay in this low growl that I can only assume is meant to be intimidating or something but is really just very inefficient. I wouldn't even mind so much if they weren't so obsessive about us "sounding off." (Yelling whenever we speak to them.)

Time passes... Tuesday

Hey! I got that package from Amazon.com and your letter from July 4. It is so encouraging to hear from home. It'd be really encouraging to read those books too; unfortunately, all reading material is confiscated here! But I can't tell you how much they meant to me. Thanks for going out of your way to find one I haven't read and getting a brand new release! I'm always near tears (happy ones) when I hear from home.

Even though I still feel I should get out, I am feeling much more that God wants me to continue getting physically fit and mentally disciplined here. I will take what I learn back to civilian life.

When I come back, you will find a brand new JB — full of energy and happy again. Of course, don't expect much the first two days. I'll probably just want to relax and recover and probably whine, but after that I'll be fine. I love running. I want to join a gym. U of D has one. On the downside, I'll probably eat all the food in the house.

I think that God wanted me to remember all I had and instill drive and get me to seek Him of course, but the first one I think was the key. I think that joining the army was the second stupidest thing I ever did. The stupidest was quitting church. I think about going back to Grace (double entendre) all the time.

You know I'd never have had to do the number two stupid thing if I hadn't done number one. Some lessons are costly. But it's better in the long run. Now I want to know how strong I can get. Of course, right now I'm getting weaker. We don't get enough time to rebuild these first two weeks but in 8 – 10 days I should be getting stronger. When I'm plain clothes again, I think I'll adopt a slightly less frantic workout program.

July 30, 2001

Dear Mom,

Well, I've been continuing to rip my hair out (metaphorically) and prayerfully considering (in that order, cycling repeatedly) whether I should stay or go. I've finally decided I should try to leave. If I can't then I will assume God has me in His holy web. If I get out, praise God that I was given this opportunity to change.

Everyday I wake up and can't believe I joined! If only I had known or could have figured out how to do the right thing. I mean, I kinda knew in the back of my head, but it never clicked. And now I'm stuck here. Ugh.

JB

Speaking of workouts, we had another three-mile run today. This time I stayed right at the beginning. I forced myself not to fall out like I did last run. It felt so good to have completed it! Of course, that means the next workout is going to be push-ups and sit-ups until exhaustion. It's a real killer. Fortunately, today we had a little time to recover and build muscle — because we haven't gotten smoked all day! (Frantic searching for a piece of wood to knock on...)

I definitely haven't begun to get any bigger, but I'm sure I will if I keep this up. I really almost want to complete BCT now, but I am more and more certain that I can excel and distinguish myself better in civilian life.

Mom, I would like to work on a book with you too. I think if at breakfast every morning we plan out a halfday of work for me to do on it we could get something done. When I'm at U of D, we could still work stuff out over the phone. And I'd come home on weekends for church and for some food, of course :-)

But I'm getting ahead of myself. Even as much as I've changed already, I've got several more weeks to push through. I still need more discipline. Well, I need to make sure this gets out.

Love,
JB

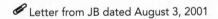

✐ Letter from JB dated August 3, 2001

Dear Mom,
Well, today was long, but it seems to have gone by quickly. I am very tired. We got smoked a couple of times, but it was all class-

"Just point it that way and pull the trigger!"

room and bay inspection. I don't seem to be recovering from the workouts well, even on light days. I don't know why I don't get stronger. Oh well, I keep trying.

I am praying for wisdom and courage. I want to talk to a DI about getting out. I need to really get up the nerve. I keep saying tomorrow. I might make it through BCT just because I never bring myself to ask about getting out.

Later

Well, I have qualified on my rifle. I am one of the top 20 shots in the whole company. I was pretty proud of myself. I shot $^{34}/_{40}$, only two short of earning an Expert Badge. I know exactly which two I should have picked up too.

Yes, I have been reading my Bible whenever I can. I bought another one as well, just in case. [Editor's Note: Just in case of what, I wonder?] I just finished Hebrews, which is now my favorite book.

Letter from JB dated August 9, 2001

Dear Home,

Well it's been a while since I have written. Partly, even mostly, I've been dead tired at lights out, but partly I've been down and haven't felt like writing.

Everyone has been great about writing me! I've been getting mail everyday. Thank you all so much!

Well, what we've been doing lately is fighting. We've practiced lots of hand-to-hand. We've used the pugil sticks (I want to buy a set of these) and bayonets. Tomorrow is the bayonet course, which should be extremely exhausting.

I had KP on Sunday and was given a piece of pie and an ice cream taco at the end. It was sublime.

Well, here is the main reason for the letter: I have finally set up a time to talk to a DI about leaving. It is tomorrow. I need lots of prayer for boldness and for God's will. I am, however, nearly certain that I will be getting out. What I will receive is called an

ELS, which probably stands for something. It is nothing literally. [Editor's Note: Tyler maintains that this is a French acronym for just fooling.] It means you were never officially in the military [Editor's Note: What? Just visiting boot camp?!] After it is complete, and if you wanted, you could re-enlist after six months. [Editor's Note: Right.]

That is my plan. I will re-enlist in the air force. (Why didn't I do that to start with?!) Probably Reserves. All I really want is college money anyway. Then I will choose a technically oriented MOS and learn some useful skills. [Editor's Note: I agree, pugil sticks and bayonets will only get one so far.]

I think the problem was that I joined the infantry. It's bad enough doing this stuff in basic. I wouldn't want to live it. I wish I'd thought to do communications or even become a mechanic. I wouldn't mind something where I learned a practical skill.

Anyway, I will probably be seeing you at the airport soon. That is an army soon. The paperwork will likely take a week or two. But I am letting you know so you can get mentally prepared. [Editor's Note: Should I tell him he doesn't have a bedroom anymore? We just moved the office into it!]

Letter from JB dated August 10, 2001

Dear Home,

Well, once again I got my hopes up and was disappointed. The drill sergeant said I wasn't doing badly enough for an ELS. I can't believe that for once, trying hard not to mess up is punishing me.

I almost wish I had been a screw-up like the private who did get ELS when he asked.

I think August 15 is the last day that I can get ELS. I'm going to talk to the DI one more time. In the meantime I will continue to pray and listen. I was so sure that my place is as a civilian. I still am partly sure, but maybe I am deluding myself. Pray hard for guidance.

Today we did the bayonet course. It was a ton of running, engaging targets, long elbow crawls on rocks, fence clearing, and moving under barbed wire. I was so tired afterward. Oh yeah, we also had some dumb classes.

Signing off,

JB

Dear Home,

Well, I was very depressed when I was told I couldn't quit, but today I am feeling much better. You know, I think I actually want to graduate now.

I'm starting to get used to the idea of going out on my own. I'm still leery of day-to-day life in my unit, but it's starting to look better. One thing the DI said is that infantry, when not in the field, often doesn't work Mondays and only works half a day on Fridays. That sounded good to me. Just pray for peace.) [Author's Note: I have no idea where this guy got his info!]

Today started out horribly. We had combat PT, which was PT in our BDUs. These boots are killers to exercise in. [Editor's Note:

In case you are wondering, he never did get that second pair of boots!] We ran all over the place carrying ammo cans, five-gallon jugs, and worst of all — each other. I had to run uphill with a 175-pound deadweight on my back. Ugh. Then we crawled on our elbows through rocks, cleared bunkers, and shoulder crawled though the mud under barbed wire. When everyone else finished, we went to the sawdust pit and wrestled. I swear it is only the thought of breakfast that gets me through PT.

But ever since then, today has been easy. It's almost like being back at the 30th. I've been trying to write as much as possible.

Well, many hours have passed since this sentence and the last. I'll just say again I am starting to feel better about the army and even a few of the guys here. A few. Don't get too excited.

I'm still going to ask for an ELS right before my time is up, but if the answer is no, so be it. I will continue to try. If we get long weekends that often anyway I might show up on my motorcycle kinda often anyway, if I can.

Hey! Luke needs a birthday present from me. Please take some of my money and buy him a gift.

I'm gonna sleep now because tomorrow is Sunday, so there is no point in mailing it now. I'll make it longer first.

It's Sunday morning now and I'm very sore from yesterday's PT. Fortunately, Sunday is a very light day. I don't have KP this time so I'll be able to attend Bible study. Since I'm sick of chapel, I've decided to try out the Pentecostal service. They have a band so maybe the music won't frustrate me so much.

Oh, I won't be coming home after graduation. I have to complete airborne school first. But, if the holdover is long enough, when I do come home for leave and hometown recruiting, it might be around Christmas, so I may be home longer and not have to take as much of my earned leave.

I've heard that there is still such a thing as extra jump pay, so Airborne will definitely be worthwhile. There is an airborne unit in Alaska. I'm seriously thinking about trying to go there. (That would negate me biking home, of course.) There is no state income tax, and residents receive one thousand to two thousand dollars a month from state surplus. That's a lot. [Editor's Note: Of course, residents spend that much a month in mosquito repellent...]

I am really starting to like some of what I hear about different bases. Plus, with my bonus I could really start to set myself up. Getting that bike paid off would be great, and I could work on saving for a car.

The army also has a program where you can take about 12 college credits over a laptop they give you and then you get to keep the computer. [Author's Note: It's crap! It's crap I tell you! That laptop and the related college course program has been my biggest army-induced headache of all time.]

Well, keep writing me lots of letters. For a few moments while I'm reading, I'm back home.

I miss you all very much. And I was about to close when I thought of some more stuff to write. Go ahead and get Tyler a present from me.

Please send more pictures! Pictures are always good!

I guess I could catch you up on some of the stuff that we have been doing for training. The last week has been bayonet fighting and hand-to-hand combat. We ran the bayonet course just a few days ago and I was so beat afterward.

We had to elbow crawl through rocks, run and attack targets, face crawl up hills and under barbed wire. Wow. After bayonet fighting we did hand-to-hand combat and grappling. It was pretty cool. I learned some dangerous stuff.

We always fight in a sawdust pit though, so we are always all scratched up and horribly dirty afterward. But it makes the breakfast taste great.

Ugh. Time lapse here. Sunday just got terrible. Some people got candy from the machine, so we spent the whole day being smoked. Then after dinner the whole company was put on K.P. Very wasteful. I was in the absolute last group out too. So I'm tired now. I'm gonna close. Tomorrow we qualify with grenades. I'm gonna fail. Maybe. I'll tell you all about it.

Love,

JB

Letter from JB dated August 21, 2001

Dear Home,

Phew, I am dead tired. We had another bivouac last night. We did our first practice movement and firing range. It involved a lot of crawling and short rushing across a sandy hill. We did it once with blanks and once with live ammo. We also threw grenades in a couple of bunkers. My left knee is so skinned up it's hard to bend it. I'm getting pretty banged up.

Enclosed in this letter you will find some information about graduation. I will make a list for you of food items to bring. Just so you know, my hopes for an ideal family pass day consists of eating out then doing really passive stuff like playing board games.

So, I'm thinking a big breakfast around 7:00 — sleeping in! [Editor's Note: My, how we've changed!] Then for lunch and dinner, we should find a cool place and have a family meal. I'd also like to all go in a huge group with a few of the guys here who have turned out to be really cool. Are you driving or flying? I hope you are driving so you can bring a cooler of food for me.

Yeah, I've made a few good friends here. One of them, Anderson, shares a great many of my interests in games, books, and music. It's amazing how much being able to talk about fun stuff has alleviated the pressure I feel! The time we spend together talking is a great escape. It is really making this time easier to bear.

Next day

We just finished our Class 11 issue. Those army greens are really sharp. But guess what? They didn't have a jacket in my size. I wasn't surprised. [Editor's Note: I wasn't either — believe me!] But everything else still looked really good. We even got a cool black trench coat and another set of leather gloves.

I have to send this now, although I have lots more to say. More later!

~JB

Letter from JB dated August 23, 2001

Dear Home,

Well tomorrow is my birthday. I'm getting my most unusual present yet: a squad assault weapon, or saw. It should be exciting. I'd still much rather be home to celebrate though.

I've finally made some good friends here. You'll meet them at graduation. One of them is very into acting and recommended a college that sounded cool. That and some training in my writing with Chris Stout might be worth something. I'll have to let that boil in the back of my head.

I've also befriended the weakest link. We share a few of the same interests. I'm trying to keep the jerks from dragging him down and at the same time push him and keep him from slacking off. He is also a new Christian. A few months maybe. He could use prayer. His name is (and this doesn't help!) Wormley.

We had our airborne physical today. They didn't bother to check my knees or spine like the card says to but they went ahead and cleared me anyway. It was kind of stupid. We were there for about five hours and we only did about 30 minutes of actual, well, stuff. They took blood too.

I miss being on top of current events back home. I'd love to get caught up politically and internationally.

This just occurred to me, please send a thimble. I have to sew my pants occasionally and the needle hurts my finger. [Editor's Note: Oh, how I'd love to see this!]

Please send pictures!

JB

Letter from JB dated August 25, 2001

Dear Home,

So how was my birthday? Considering the circumstances, it was pretty good! We only got smoked twice. But, best of all, my birthday present was a SAW — full automatic machine gun, a firing range, and a long belt of ammo! [Editor's Note: Men are from Mars.] The SAW is a very cool gun. It is heavy; and very unwieldy, but it spits out a lot of bullets. It has a built-in bipod — it is supposed to be fired in the prone position. I like it because it only takes one guy to set up, uses regular 5.56 rounds (same as the M16) and still packs a serious punch. [Editor's Note: Men are definitely from Mars.]

Sometime next week we'll fire the M204B, which is a really big gun. I don't go crazy over it like some of the guys. [Editor's Note: Words to warm a mother's heart...] To me it is too cumbersome. I like versatility. [Editor's Note: Never mind.] We'll be using the grenade-launcher attachment on our M16s soon. Talk about versatility! [Sigh...]

How are things at Grace? Is the music continuing to get better and better? How long has Pastor Seda been gone? Why exactly was he gone, anyway? I wish you could send me sermon tapes.

How is Luke? I sent him a letter to encourage him. Have you seen Nicole and Mellora? I still haven't heard from Mellora. Also, I know Tom wrote me back at 30th AG, but I still haven't received it! I know there is still a significant amount of misdirected mail floating around for me. It's like a little time warp for me to read old letters. It's actually kinda cool. It gets hard to keep events straight in my mind though.

So, now it has been 51 days of training. This is not counting the time at 30th AG. We have something like 48 days until graduation. I am past the hump now. But that is time-wise. It's going to keep getting tougher here. Tell people to please keep writing!

I have a good idea for a project for me when I get home: I

think I'd like to put in a decorative garden with a pond and stone walkway.

Oh yes, I want a tattoo when I get back. I want an infinity cross, but I can't decide where I want it. I think right in the center of my back. [Editor's Note: Groan...]

I'll write more when stuff happens.

~JB

Dear Home,

News? I've been hearing worrisome things about the U.S. deploying to Iraq again. Operation Stardust, what is it?

Hey, look on eBay and see if Star Trek figures are being sold. I'm curious to see if my collection has accrued some value. Boy, my mind has really been on hobbies lately. I guess what I need right now is something that'll pass the time and relieve some stress.

We are through the hardest part though. I can see the light at the end of the tunnel, and now I'm starting to think about stuff that I want to do when I'm allowed a life again. I don't think that's unhealthy.

Anyway, by the time you get this, I'll have talked to you the day before yesterday :-)

~JB

Dear Home,

I had first fireguard tonight. The fire alarm went off! It was this weak, little, asthmatic duck sound. I thought it was a malfunction at first. When it didn't stop, I leapt into action. I threw on the lights and started shouting at everyone to get out. "Don't waste time with your shoes! You want to die in a fiery Hell with your hands fused to your half-laced boots?" "I don't care if you are in a towel, that's less clothing to catch on fire!" It was great.

This is week 9. After we complete it we are done with all the "basic" part of basic. We start doing all the "cool-guy" stuff, as one of our DIs likes to call AIT (Advanced Infantry Training). As long as I can pass the phase-3 test, which I am not worried about, I should be rolling downhill from there. Each day is about momentum — if I made it this far, I can go all the way. That's my new motto. [Editor's Note: This is way preferable to some of his earlier mottoes!] [Author's Note: Such as parasites are people too?]

October 5 is the Crossed Rifle Ceremony. That is our last week of training — basically the month of September is all we have left. Our last day of PT is in a couple of weeks. One week is spent just on prepping for FTX. The light at the end of the tunnel is getting brighter. Just pray it isn't the headlight of a freight train coming my way.

Well, shift is over. I gotta go.

Love,

JB

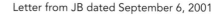

Dear Home,

I figured I'd fail grenades because I throw like a girl. But after practicing a bunch, I got it down and passed all but one of the obstacles. I don't really like grenades much; I'm much better with my M16. I finally got my second set of boots today! We had a quarter master refit. You have no idea how good it feels to have a full issue of gear. Well, I am still missing my laundry bag — but I have more socks than I know what to do with. Maybe that evens out cosmically.

~JB

Dear Home,

Today we had our phase-3 testing. It went really well for me. I got a go on everything the first time around and I moved quickly enough that I got it all done. Quite a few people have to go back tomorrow to finish or retest.

The night firing was really cool. We used M16s-A4s for that. They have places to mount a laser light and a scope that lets you see everything in kind of a green haze. We used tracers too. It was like watching *Star Wars*.

The grenade course was pretty straightforward. We went

from one place to another, throwing grenades at bunkers and trucks, into mortar pits, etc. We also got to throw two live ones. You literally felt the earth beneath you jolt when they went off. We also messed around with some smoke grenades and an extremely powerful incendiary grenade. It burnt all the way through five inches of steel.

The land mines were pretty boring. We just used dummies to learn on. We did get to watch two real ones go off.

It was pretty much the same with the rocket launcher. They put in this stupid little adapter so we had this big ol' bazooka firing stupid little 9mm rounds. I was one of the ones considered to shoot the live munitions because I fired so well. I didn't get to, but it was still nice to be one of the best.

I can't believe how close we are to graduation. In two weeks we'll be starting FTX. That is going to be a really long week. The last three days the drills have been saying that we won't get any sleep. I don't know if that is true or not because the drills have made a lot of empty threats, but it's still a frightening prospect.

Well, I keep falling asleep writing this so I'm gonna sign off for now. Only 32 days until graduation!

~JB

Dover responds to the terrorist attacks

By ERIN KOSNAC, JEFF BROWN
Staff Writers

As the horrors of Tuesday morning's terrorist attacks began to reach Dover, the city and the state of Delaware took their own precautions. Assuming the maximum level of security at Dover Air Force Base was among them.

Dover AFB spokesman TSgt. Mitch Gettle said the base had gone to ThreatCon Delta, the military's highest level of security. Only authorized Department of Defense identification card holders are being allowed on the base for the foreseeable future.

"Our main interest right now is to protect our resources and our people," Gettle said, adding the base has not received any specific threat to its security. The base is being proactive to guard against possible threats.

"We're in a very fluid environment right now," Gettle said, "Our leaders on base are doing everything that's necessary."

Gettle added the base mortuary, which normally handles large numbers of casualties after accidents or terrorist acts, has not been activated.

Conferring with state and federal public safety officials, Gov. Ruth Ann Minner ordered nonessential state employees to go home, schools to close and recommended businesses do the same.

"Though there has not been a threat to Delaware and there is no reason for panic, I want to take every precaution. This is a time when families should be together," Minner said in a press release Tuesday. "Every individual should be very aware of their surroundings at work, as they leave work if they do so, and at home. Again this is not a time for panic, but it is a time for caution."

All school districts and City of Dover offices closed in response to the national situation.

As the toll of this tragedy remained uncertain, Bishop Michael A. Saltarelli, bishop of the Catholic Diocese of Wilmington released a statement.

"...I call on the people of Delaware and Maryland's Eastern Shore to pray with me for the innocent victims of this attack and their families, for the American people and our leaders..."

09/11/200

Dear Home,

They say that September 11 will live alongside December 7 in infamy. I have heard and overheard a lot. They say that there were more casualties today than at Pearl Harbor. I have heard that two huge towers that I saw not too long ago with some good friends are now a pile of rubble and bodies. I have heard that the army wing of the Pentagon was destroyed — but Generals Shelton and Shinseki were not present. That fortress that is the State Department is completely gone as far as I know. And the final slap was delivered when Camp David was hit. I don't even know what they mean by "hit." And the last thing I heard is that this is one of three planned strikes on the U.S.

We are only a few baby steps from declaring war. All we need to do is find out who to declare war on. This is probably the scariest day of my life. I have heard all kinds of rumors: "If something goes down we'll deploy three days after graduation." "We may go on alert and they can send anyone here as long as they have qualified on their rifles." "We know who did it." "We'll never know." "Delta Force and the third Ranger battalion are already prepping."

It's like the whole world went crazy in a couple of hours. The last news we got was around 1300 — then the drill sergeants disappeared. I don't know if anything else has gone down since then. I am anxiously awaiting mail and news for tonight but not really expecting it. We didn't get mail yesterday either.

But all that and our training and PT and chow all seem really secondary right now. I'm sorry I can't really think of anything to tell you about now. The specter of war looms, and all I know is that I want to get as much out of every piece of training that I can get. That may be what keeps me alive in a few weeks/months.

I don't want you to worry about me though. I am in God's hands and it is His choice where I go. And I promise you — I will come home from any combat I am sent to.

Please keep me, the victims, the president, and the nations at risk in prayer. PLEASE send some kind of condensed news reports as you can. I love you guys. See you soon.

~JB

Letter from JB dated September 12, 2001

Dear Home,
This letter is being written hours later. Everyone is in bed and I

September 12, 2001

Dear Home,

...So, here's what's been going on. We had our five-mile Eagle run yesterday. Too easy — we had it done in 43:10. Wish we'd gone around 35:00 or less. But the entire company minus only 5 percent must pass the run so they keep it slow. Correction. That should read only 5 percent can fall out or go on sick call and not pass the run or the company does not graduate.

Tomorrow at 0345 we are stepping out for a quick eight-mile road march. Not a whole lot of fun. It's going to be all day buddy-team movement. Then the night infiltration course, which is crawling under live machine gun fire...

am guarding them. A good thief could be behind me though as I am concentrating more on this letter than on those numbskulls around me. Not my fault if they leave their lockers open anyway.

Today was really scary. Make no mistake. But one of the drills called a formation to dispel rumor — which really helped. Camp David was not hit. Nobody is deploying anywhere and training will continue as normal. However, America is in a serious state, and we are on a further news blackout. Training is going to be super serious. I just hope everyone can get that into their skulls.

So, here's what's been going on. We had our five-mile Eagle run yesterday. Too easy — we had it done in 43:10. Wish we'd gone around 35:00 or less. But the entire company minus only 5 percent must pass the run so they keep it slow. Correction. That should read only 5 percent can fall out or go on sick call and not pass the run or the company does not graduate.

Tomorrow at 0345 we are stepping out for a quick eight-mile road march. Not a whole lot of fun. It's going to be all day buddy-team movement. Then the night infiltration course, which is crawling under live machine gun fire. Then we bivouac and ride back here. I'm not real excited about tomorrow, but it'll probably make the week go by faster.

I am still concerned about the state of, well, everything right now. The drill sergeant said everything has changed overnight. Anything that happens — especially any statements the president issues would be really nice to read.

For the meantime I am okay. There's no reason to start worrying now. There may be a time to worry later, but there just as likely may not. Forget about the future until it happens.

Looking forward to hearing from you.

Tiredly,

JB

Dear Home,

I received more letters from you on Thursday. We hadn't received mail in a while because of bivouacs and stuff. It was good to hear from you guys.

I'm still going to the Pentecostal service. It's better than nothing, I guess. I really miss Grace, especially getting a message with some real depth.

Well, this is the unpleasant part. As you know, on the 11th a whole lot of bad stuff happened and the world totally changed. President Bush has said that he has declared war on terrorists and anyone who harbors or helps them. If we start deploying for war, the infantry goes. On October 12, I will be part of the infantry.

Don't start worrying now though. It is probably equally likely that I will not deploy or see any combat. [Author's Note: Ha! Ha Ha!] Also, they will not pull us out of basic or anything crazy like that. You can be sure that I am getting the training I need to survive and kill the enemy if I am called to do so.

Although I do want revenge, I'm not desirous of combat and war, and I do not hope for battle. Whatever comes, I will do my duty and be as prepared as I possibly can. President Bush has told everyone who wears a uniform to get ready. We are here getting ready. Don't worry about me. There are lots of us. Many may not go. If we do all go, there will be tons of us. We have a great number of allies too. Heck, even Russia has said they'll cover our back on this one. So I'll be there with plenty of battle buddies.

Don't start worrying. [Editor's Note: I guess I have a certain reputation along those lines.] There is no need. I am perfectly safe and continuing to train. FTX is coming up in less than two weeks and I will learn tons there. In less than a month I'll be seeing you guys.

For now, war or no war, deployment or regular duty, it's all up in the air. Things will continue as normal. But start praying a lot. Please put me in the bulletin for prayer as well. Things may go totally smoothly but they could also go very bad very quickly. So pray.

By the way, for some reason we are watching a movie instead of using the phone. It's *Air Force One*. [Editor's Note: Interesting choice!] I'll write more later. Things are going well here. I love you all very much! See you in 27 days.

~JB

Dear friends and family,

This letter from JB has been sitting on my desk for several days, unbeknownst to me, buried under a pile of papers. Bob, Tyler and I are leaving very early next Wednesday for graduation. If any of you that were thinking of going want to know our hotel info, please email us. We will be there Thursday for the family day ceremony and will stay through Sunday as long as he has leave. Thanks for all your prayers and letters! It has been an

"You said a night mission tonight, right guys?"

amazing thing to watch his growth through this process. God is good! We continue to covet your prayers for him during this next phase of training.

Blessings,
Maggie

September 27, 2001

Dear Home,
Well, here is my last letter home before FTX. [Editor's Note: This is some sort of weeklong field exercise under very tough conditions.]

09/11/2001   45

We are stepping out at 0400 for our 15-mile road march. It is going to be an intense week. Let me say a few things before I start rambling about FTX. Don't send any more letters after October 6. That should leave plenty of time for them to get here before graduation. After that wait for my new address. Please add one can of cashews and one bag of chocolate stuffed Oreos to the food list.

Have you made reservations at a hotel yet? I really hope you get a suite so that we can cook and stuff. [Editor's Note: We?] ...And have actual separate rooms. That really appeals to me now. One room with 55 guys really stinks after a while. A short while.

Well, let me tell you about FTX now. Wake up is at 0200. We step out at 0400. That day won't end until 0300. It's gonna be rough. The road march will be a little over 15 miles. Our rucks were way lighter than standard load when we packed the first time. However, that was only the first list. Our rucks are overflowing now. I don't think I could add a toothbrush if I wanted to. [Editor's Note: Does this mean he has NO toothbrush?]

Fourth Squad (my squad) was designated the special weapons squad — just like in a real unit. I got issued a rocket launcher.) I was kinda hoping for a SAW but I feel pretty cool being one of only two guys here who can do anything about a tank or a Bradley showing up. The other guy is my battle buddy — who is, with all intended affection, a total box of rocks — so it's pretty much up to me.

Okay, it's naptime. I'll write more tonight.

Our platoon is pretty well equipped this cycle. They are trying to make it as close to combat load as possible. We are packing four 240BS, six SAWs, and six grenade launchers. We also have two huge radio systems (the antenna sticks three feet out of the ruck!), and one small radio per squad. Then we've got night vision scopes for all automatic weapons. We've got claymore mines and tons of ammo. We look much better than any other company going on FTX.

Hopefully we'll get mail one last time before we step out. It'd be nice to have some words from home in my head before I leave. Anyway. On Wednesday we had our final PT test. It was about 38 degrees outside. Our uniform was a long sleeve shirt and shorts. It was absolutely horrible. I still managed to run 14:10 but I collapsed afterwards. I could hardly breathe! That's the second time my asthma has really interfered. It takes really cold air to do so. [Editor's Note: Please pray. Thirty-eight degrees is not nearly as cold as some places he may be sent!] I think I'll be okay though. As bad as it was, it wasn't like it used to be back home.

I did 79 sit-ups in two minutes. One hundred percent on the PT test is 78. I was pleased. I only did 43 push-ups. Forty-two is 60 percent and the cut-off for graduation, so that was close. I'll keep getting higher at my unit.

Well, so far it looks like my leave (the two days after graduation) is a go. Also, unless things get really ugly, I'll be home for Christmas. That would be nice. Maybe I can make it to the New Year's Eve party.

I've decided against OCS for now, partly because I want to fight when it's my time and partly because you can make more money in the long run if you go in with a higher NCO rank.

Ranger school is almost for sure not an option anymore. Lots of people are having it taken away. I will still get Airborne though. I was really hoping to call before FTX but it doesn't look good. Oh well. It is really close to graduation. Only six more training days.

Have you got up with Sue and Dwayne? I really hope Luke

comes down on the 12th. Let my friends know anyone is welcome to come — Mellora, Nicole, whoever can come. Relatives too!

~JB

Hi All,

He did it! He really really did it! Just a note to let you know that Bob, Tyler, and I got back late last night from Ft. Benning, Georgia. We had a great time with JB. I'll give you a rundown of our days.

Thursday: After making our way through the security check where our truck was inspected, we followed the security checkpoints guarded by soldiers and barbed wire to JB's building. We then sat in a large classroom and listened to a lieutenant colonel explain a little about the last 14 weeks of training. They showed a video of some of the things the guys had done. (All guys — no women in the infantry!) He remarked that this overflowing roomful of parents and friends was the largest he'd had at a parent's day event. I'm sure everyone had the events of 9/11 on their minds.

Diane Gorman and her two sons, who are now stationed in Alabama, met us and were able to watch the ceremony with us. It was great having special friends to share it with!

Then we went outside and sat in bleachers as they began the "Turning Blue" ceremony. This is when they get the Infantryman's Blue Cord on their shoulder. Bob was able to place it there. He was the first to spot JB — standing tall in the back. I hardly recognized him. Then the soldiers were released on a pass until 8 P.M. that night. It was so amazing to see him standing there in his uniform — taller, tanner, and more fit and serious than before.

On our way out of the barracks we had to stop at the PX so he could buy something. He hopped back in the car with a large bag of M&M's! (We hadn't brought any of the food on base because we were told they would be searching cars and we needed to make it as easy as possible by having an empty car — which we did!)

We went directly out to lunch at Macon Road Bar-b-Cue (Thanks Stephanie and Andy!) and enjoyed a big meal. From the time we picked him up until we brought him back, JB ate almost nonstop.) Then we went back to the hotel and he happily put on his "civvies" and began eagerly going through all the goodies from home. He was excited to see the homemade treats from Janice and Linda and he dug right into them. He opened his graduation presents — books from us, money, and a really cool knife from Me-Ma and George. Next on his list was a trip to Wal-Mart where he was able to pick out his birthday present from us. (A Game Boy Advance was his choice.)

Back at the hotel room we talked and he ate and we talked and he ate. Dinner was pizza delivered and then it was time to head back to the barracks.

Graduation on Friday was awesome. Dwayne and Susan Williams, great buddies for many years and surrogate parents to the boys, made the trip from Atlanta. We sat in the bleachers on the parade grounds and waited while the band played. Then we heard what sounded like a bunch of bombs going off. There were smoke bombs and flares, music blasts, and then a Bradley armored personnel carrier (to me it was a tank) came roaring out of the woods. Out jumped a bunch of soldiers in combat uniforms and weapons. They did maneuvers across the field, the Bradley roared across the field and did a wheelie, then they all jumped back in and went flying back into the woods. Way cool!

Then there were the speeches. The band played, and then the second Battalion marched onto the field and were officially graduated. They marched off to the side and we were allowed fifteen minutes with him. Next we sat and waited a really long time while JB was "outprocessed." Turns out there is a waiting list for the waiting list for airborne school, and instead of going right there they have to hang out here in the barracks for a few more days. So all the stuff they packed up has to be put back.

Anyway, we then had JB until Sunday at 5:00 P.M. We spent a lot of time eating, meeting up with his friends and their families at, oddly enough, restaurants and malls with food courts. We also played lots of games with Sue and Dwayne, talking and eating some more. Unfortunately for the rest of us, only JB can manage to eat like that and not show it...We played Scrabble and Acquire and Masterpiece and talked and talked and ate some more. We also went to the Infantryman's Museum on base, which the guys thought was really cool. I was having back and leg trouble and spent that time recouping, asleep in the truck. JB also managed to get some time in at a music store and a hobby shop. Sunday he wanted to go to church so we found a PCA church and went. The message was solid, but the music was, let's say, really old fashioned. (To my GPC friends: after the youth group sang the one and only contemporary chorus while clapping in time to the music, the pastor did say he thought it was okay to clap!)

JB still has some regrets about joining but is very resigned to it and wants to make the best of it. He has definitely grown up a lot — although in many ways he is just the same. (For instance, he called us tonight and asked if we'd seen his wallet!)

Many guys in his battalion were sent on to bases where they will be deployed to Korea or to "somewhere in Asia." He and his friends and about two dozen other guys are going to airborne school first. After that he will find out where he will be stationed. He's pretty much decided not to go for Rangers. After hearing first hand what he's already been through I can't say I blame him. He just isn't a Ranger kind of guy. [Author's Note: There's a saying in the army: There are smart soldiers, and there are strong soldiers, and each of them can get the job done.] There are several specialties that appeal to him but unfortunately since he isn't going on to Rangers he is stuck with infantry for two years. After that he can try and change. I asked what his specialty was and he said, "11 Bravo." That means straight-legged infantry. In other words, he is the infantry of the infantry, the grunt of the grunts. His specialty will be walking. But he figures God has him there for a purpose, and he is okay with that.

He called tonight since he was allowed to — he'd only had two phone passes the whole 14 weeks of training. (BTW, most only go 9 weeks, infantry however goes for 14.) He'd been limping the whole weekend we were with him and he went yesterday and had his leg checked out. Seems he's pulled a flexor muscle in his hip or something like that. They gave him orders to have no PT for a week. Normally that would be good, but he's already had no PT for one week and says he's getting out of shape. Two, tomorrow is the PT test to see if you can go on to airborne. If he doesn't take it, who knows how long he'll have to wait for another chance. So he plans on taking it and asks for prayer that he'll pass it and not further damage his leg.

09/11/2001

If he passes tomorrow, he'll go to airborne holding for about a week and then will start airborne school (still at Ft. Benning). School lasts three weeks. After that he should know where he'll be assigned next. Then he's supposed to get two weeks to go to his hometown and work part-time with his recruiter. ("Thank you for finishing basic, here's your perk: two weeks of light duty while being at home.") Then he has 10 days leave coming. If all works out, he may get this time in December and be home for Christmas. That would be great!

After listening to the officers there, other soldiers, and JB himself, I realize the whole thing was a lot harder than I even dreamed. Bob and I are so thankful to each of you for your prayers, cards, letters, and encouragement both to him and to us during the last four months. The 10 pounds of mail he received really helped keep him going. He told us he received the second most mail of anyone of the 50 guys in his barracks!! He said it was the letters he looked forward to almost as much — and sometimes more than — chow time!

He has no address right now. When he does, I'll pass it on. But even though you can't write, please continue your prayers on his behalf. Spiritually, he is doing better, but he freely admits he isn't doing much Bible reading or having much prayer time. He knows he needs to but... So if you think of it, pray he continues to grow in the understanding and love of the Lord. Bob and I are sure it was prayer warriors that really made the difference these last months. We have seen such positive changes in our son and pray that God will continue to do a good work in him. Thank you all!

We'll let you know what happens with airborne school when

we know. Bob is going to scan in some graduation pictures and email them when he gets a chance.

P.S. I have to tell you — he did finally get boots — two weeks before graduation! They were a size 11. He wears an 8½. But right at the end they were allowed to exchange any uniforms for different sizes. (Most of the guys lost weight and needed smaller pants.) JB was the only one to exchange his boots. He said he didn't say a word, leaving the supply sergeant wondering....

~Maggie Hogan

Letter from JB dated January 8, 2002

Dear Everybody,

As you know I joined the army in June. I have completed basic training at Ft. Benning, Georgia, and have become a qualified infantryman. (I'm the man with the gun who ties up the loose ends after the air force is done with their special effects displays.)

After BCT I was training at the airborne school hoping to earn my Jump Wings and be qualified to hurtle my body out of an aircraft cruising 150 mph at 1250 feet, suspended by some canvas and a few bits of string. (This is worth promotion points — not to be confused with IQ points. We're jumping out of a perfectly good airplane here, people!)

However, I developed shin splints, which progressed into two stress fractures in my right leg during the runs at the school. This made it impossible to complete the training. (It also hurt like heck!) I was then shuffled over to worldwide holdover awaiting orders to anywhere in the world.

As irony would have it, I received orders to stay right here at Ft. Benning. I am assigned to a mechanized infantry unit, which means I'll be riding in the back of a BFV (Bradley fighting vehicle), hoping it doesn't stop. When it stops, you have to jump out and start shooting. Also, you have to do a ton of maintenance and mechanical work on it, but it also means you don't have to walk places.

I am looking forward to being fully healed and getting back to work. I am excited to finally start doing "real" army stuff. It should be fun.

Please continue to pray for me as I really have no idea what I'm getting into. Your letters have meant a lot to me and once I get an address and my computer I can resume correspondence with you. I look forward to hearing from everybody.

~JB

City taxes going up

By JEFF BROWN
Staff Writer

Residents in the city of Dover may soon be writing bigger checks to pay their electric and water bills, and property owners will be sending more money to the city coffers under a new draft city budget, adopted by City Council during a recent three-day negotiating session.

Under the new budget, the average residential electric bill will go up by about $17 per year, while the combined average water and wastewater rates will increase by about $58 annually, based on a usage of 7,000 gallons per month.

The draft budget was approved by a 6 – 2 vote. The entire new budget tops out at about $96.9 million, said City Manager Anthony J. DePrima.

The draft budget, presented by DePrima at the beginning of the special budget session on May 14, included the rate increases and property tax adjustments in an effort to increase the city's revenues, which have not grown as much as city officials had hoped.

The decline in revenue came as a result of what DePrima called a "difficult budget environment" this fiscal year in which the city's revenues have not kept pace with increases in the city's expenditures.

DePrima addressed part of this concern by ordering city department heads to trim almost $1.1 million dollars from the draft budget even before it was presented to the council.

The good news, DePrima said, is that there will be no decrease in the services the city provides to its citizens. There are also no new fees, he said.

During their deliberations, council members voted down a proposal to eliminate the city's trash fee, which was adopted by a controversial vote early last year. Ritter and Speed had made their opposition to the fee an integral part of their successful 2001 election campaigns, and both cast the only votes in favor of doing away with it.

The trash fee is the city's fifth-largest revenue earner, bringing in over $850,000 annually. DePrima said that if council had managed to eliminate the fee, the city might have had to lay off between 15 and 20 employees to make up the difference.

KUWAIT

Operation Sandbox

Letter from JB dated May 21, 2002

Holy Cow Everyone,

I'm in Kuwait! It is incredible. Already I have gone from *whoa, this is awesome!* to *one more day of this and I'm killing myself!* and back again. Let me start from the beginning.

It all started first thing Sunday morning. I was tired and not really in a "let's deploy!" mood. But I staggered out of bed and dragged all 155 pounds of gear (my body weight incidentally) to the company area. Then we did all sorts of stuff that I don't recall. I was tired and that seems a lifetime ago. We then filed into the rec center to await buses to Lawson Army Airfield (at Ft. Benning). Even though we had already stowed duffle bags and rucksacks I still had 60 pounds of junk to wear. [Editor's Note: I wonder how many pounds of that was in the form of books?]

The plane was a Boeing 777. Talk about unbelievably cool! Each seat had a built in TV and remote. There are three columns of three seats each, plus first class. It would have been very pleasant had there been no soldiers on it. I watched *Frasier* and some movies.

The flight was very long and messed with your head. Between sleeping at odd times, the 7-hour time change, 15 hours of flight, and 3 hours of delays I was thoroughly messed up by the time we got in the country. We arrived in Kuwait International Airport at about 1730 local time on the 20th. It was my first experience with time travel. It was strangely anticlimactic. Of course, seven hours isn't exactly a huge leap.

The airport isn't too shoddy. We got off the planes and right onto buses. The buildings are ugly orange in color but in good repair. There are lines of hedges, trees (palms and short bushy ones), and grass! So far Kuwait is mocking my expectations. Board buses. Sleep. Exacerbate already bad jet lag.

It's 1930. Not the year. We only traveled in time for seven hours, remember? We arrived at Camp Doha.

Serious whoa! Warehouses. Military vehicles everywhere. Not as hot as I expected. [Editor's Note: Not then. He's since called us once and reported temperatures of 137 and 140 degrees!] Nice breeze. Smells like that little beach by Me-Ma's house. I don't know why.

Briefing received. Lots of stupid clichés and militarisms. Got it. We've heard this all before.

We are shown to our vehicles. Mine has two serious problems. Number one, my cooling fan rotates about as quickly as...as...something notorious for revolving slowly. The Earth, maybe.

But most worrisome is my engine access hatch. This is a hydraulic lift cover that raises to expose the engine components.

Mine takes about 15 seconds to open and 7½ minutes to close. Already I'm having visions like this:

"Hogan, we're halting. Go check your fluids."

"Roger," replies our hero.

"Whirrrrr..." says the hatch.

Private First Class Hogan (who just got promoted on June 15) begins checks.

"Boom!" goes the artillery.

"We're taking fire! Get in and close the hatch, let's go!"

"Tick...tick...tick..." says the hatch moving so slowly it is unobservable to the naked eye.

"Yeah, tell the lieutenant. We're gonna be about 7½ minutes behind them," says PFC Hogan.

"Darn! Well, Hogan. We're gonna have to rely on your powers in the Force to push those shells away."

"Roger."

So, I'm not exactly thrilled with Bravo 13 right now. But I finished my vehicle PMCS and PLUT. We received BII, SKO, asked about PLL and were denied CRTT. After LNTT the TCs set up our SP and we were almost done. (Bonus game: Guess which acronyms I totally made up!)

The final task at Camp Doha was to load the Bradleys onto the HET trucks. This was terrifying. The boarding ramps were at about a 45-degree angle steep and about as wide as the tracks. It would not have been hard to tip over. When we finally loaded all the vehicles, the drivers hopped into the cab section of the truck, but everyone else got on buses.

Nice highway. Pretty lights. Sleep.

Kaboom! The truck lunges violently off the road and into the dusty side paths. Due to the extreme vibration I give up all hope of sleep. Foolishly I decide to watch the road. My driver dodges the small divots by hurtling directly into gaping potholes. I swear we went airborne.

It became a free for all once we hit the side roads. Cutting each other off, passing on the "shoulder," foregoing the road altogether in favor of the wilderness. It was wild.

About 1 km from our outpost we stopped. The Bradleys would go the rest of the way under their own power. The sun is beginning to rise. It's leering at us. "Give me eight hours and I'll have you crying for mommy," it says.

1943 hours, same day
Time to sleep.

1321 hours, next day
We arrive in the kabal. Our tents are okay. There are 12 men in each. They've got a tube running across the top to cool them off when the wind blows. There is a double door airlock system to keep the dust down. But the battle against dust isn't winnable. The Kuwaiti desert is not sand, it is dirt. Endless nasty dirt. And it blows all over. We have to clean our weapons three times a day just from walking around.

So far the work hasn't been too bad. Filling sand bags stinks, but they are relatively smart about when and for how long we do that. We have also worked a bit on the Brads but nothing major.

Breakfast this morning was canned Mexican barf eggs. It was...filling. Lunch was an MRE.

This place isn't so bad, only very dull. I'm looking forward to correspondence from you all. Should you feel so inclined, you can send me baby wipes, Gatorade powder, breakfast bars, photographs, anything! This isn't basic, and we are allowed to have stuff. Packages should be shoebox size.

More to follow as stuff happens.

~JB

P.S. Hendershot (the little red and white puppy Mellora sent me) says it's hot and he hates it here.

Holy Cow I am in Kuwait everybody!

Hello again from the stupidest place in the world to have a country — the geological equivalent of a dust bin, the land that's given me ashy dry skin, a pay raise, and a rash in an unmentionable place but not a serious attitude: Kuwait.

This is much closer to a true letter from the field than the last. I am writing by the light of a blue lantern about two by two inches inside my closed hatch. If it didn't stink so bad it'd be kinda cool.

What are we doing right now? We are pulling gate guard. The only entrance to Kabal New Jersey is protected by two Bradleys and a squad of dismounted infantry. With no ammo. Okay, technically we have ammo — 30 rounds in a mag. With tape over the top. Two pieces. In a closed Ziploc bag. In our left cargo pocket. With both buttons done. Yeah, I feel ready to rumble.

Anyway, this vehicle search/gate guard is a three-day stint and I decided to make it worth something. Basically we prevent anyone not on *the list* from entering. We use a simple process of confusion, blunder, and miscommunication to accomplish this.

The idea is that everyone pulls 2 hours on and 4 hours off for 72 hours, but fortunately the list got screwed up and I had most of Sunday off. I failed to report this error to command. But the Cosmic Forces of Malignancy (some people mistake them for justice) must have seen this because the colonel came by and tacked on another 24 hours because someone was missing their mask. Oh well, it's not so bad.

Okay, some miscellaneous stuff for your information and some simply for my own amusement. First off, as of right now, mail seems to take approximately five to six days to arrive here. (This is less than the previously assumed four weeks for those of you who favored the liberal arts in school.) [Editor's Note: I believe he is referring to me here. Harumph.]

The practical function of this is that you will receive more frequent and up-to-date communiqués from yours truly as it won't seem like a waste to write. Also, you can send more perishable items like cookies. Mmmmm...cookies!

Other interesting bits: MWR has the first morale phones in and we might start calls for our platoon as soon as Tuesday. [Editor's Note: They did and he did.] I think I'll go ahead and give you my wish list (cookies) now because I'm thinking about it.

1. Cookies
2. Baby wipes!!! At least a billion!
3. Flyswatters — I'm ready for some serious anthropoid vengeance.
4. Gatorade powder.
5. Cans of EZ Cheez.
6. Whatever — anything from home is cool!
7. Flip-flops
8. Disposable cameras

Well, I was kind of lazy this past week and never got past the "meaning to write" stage and into the "where is my stupid notebook, anyway?" stage. Fortunately, nothing really happens around here anyway. I mean, plenty of stuff happens, but no things happen, you know?! But that's okay.

We have a general routine starting to emerge. Sunday is the start of the workweek. We do our full vehicle checks in the morning. Unless we are busy doing what I like to think of as "numbskull games." We usually shut down from about 10 A.M. to 4 P.M. You can read, sleep, play games, whatever. In the evening we'll usually fill more sandbags until we decide the day is over. Then it's chill time.

I've tried to keep a journal, but it's too boring for that. Hopefully it will stay that way. Out here, boring means nothing crazy is going on. I like it that way. I might not come back with any exciting stories, but I won't be short any appendages.

Today we got to go to Camp Doha, which was huge. I bought a new CD. It was nice to be around buildings and air conditioning but there wasn't much to do. I'll end this letter now since I've run out of words. I'll write more as it transpires.

~JB

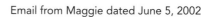

Dear Family,

Thought I'd send out a JB update since he just called and now I can't get back to sleep :-)

Yes, you read that first line correctly. He called! Actually, he called once earlier this week but it was just a couple of minutes and a lousy connection. This morning (4 A.M. our time) he called from Camp Doha and it was a great connection. In fact, I answered it quite groggily and someone said laughingly, "You sound sleepy. Why aren't you up yet?" I thought it was a bad practical joke at first. It was so good to hear his voice — I really didn't expect to get to talk to him until his tour is over (Maybe by Christmas?)

Anyway, he has the day off today, and they took him by truck to this very well-established camp about one and a half hours away from the outpost he's in. He sounded great!

What's it like in NJ? (That's what they call his outpost :-)

They are in a small tent compound that they are building onto every day. The food is not horrible. They eat one MRE a day and the rest is prepared there.

Their tasks are as follows:
- Fill sand bags. Really — they do a lot of this.
- Take out trash. (Some things never change :-)
- Do exercises — since JB drives a Bradley he must also do routine checks on it everyday. The heat is not unbearable inside when he is working in it — as long as he leaves the hatch open.

They have a good breeze there. But, when doing maneuvers, it's all closed up. Did I mention it's hot there? Yesterday it was 140!

He sleeps in a ten-man tent. They take off during the hottest hours of the day. (Since there is no a/c I can't imagine sleeping in that tent in that heat.) He was pretty sick the first week he got there with a stomach thing, and he is just starting to get his appetite back. He sounded really good this morning.

It's hard, he said, but he can handle it. Chapel service is supposed to begin there in the next week. He is looking forward to it.

He's taken a few pictures of sunsets and the local residents: large lizards the size of dogs. He can't get too close to them because they run back down into their holes in the ground. He thinks they are about four feet long.

On the home front I told him we are still working with his recruiter to try and get his sign-up bonus. This is a considerable amount of money he is owed, and the army lost his paperwork. If we don't get results next week, we will take this to Senator Biden. (He's the head of the Armed Forces Committee and his office is not far from here.) I forgot to tell him the motorcycle place called and his bike is finally repaired :-)

I sent him a box today. He needed baby wipes — lots of them! He's also requested cookies but I haven't gotten to that yet. Chocolate would not be a good idea! Cards, pictures of anything and anybody, and clippings from papers and magazines — news, weird stuff, funny stuff, inspirational stuff would all be greatly appreciated.

But mainly, please remember him in your prayers for spiritual growth and physical safety and anything else that comes to mind when you think of him. Thanks to so many of you who have faithfully prayed for him since last June when he first enlisted. Can you believe it's almost been a year? God has been so merciful toward him!

Blessings,
Maggie

Just got off the phone with JB. He was able to use the phone in his camp because at 2 p.m. his time there is usually no line. (Too hot then in the tent to stand there and talk!) At the comfortable time of day there is always a long line. He said there are three or four companies there. (If any of you know how many is in a company, let me know. Just curious.)

He sounded great! Last night he'd gotten through to Luke, which he greatly enjoyed.

They have a little px set up in their camp now where he can buy Gatorade powder. His engine hatch is fixed, and they aren't sandbagging anymore. It's kind of funny to think about what makes him happy now :-)

They spend the cooler parts of the day doing training exercises or pulling guard duty. Chapel hasn't begun yet, but a Bible study has started. Unfortunately, he's been on guard duty every time. He was very pleased to receive the Bible study materials that Jacquie Posley mailed.

Speaking of mail, he says if someone sends him something priority, he usually receives it in six days. The outgoing mail, however, is much slower because evidently they wait until they have a large batch before the letters are shipped out. He says it is harder to write now because his only free time is during the intense heat of the day.

It does cool off considerably at night and the cooling tubes in his tent work well. But they have off in the afternoon because it is too hot to do anything.

He's looking forward to June 15 because he gets his one-year promotion then (with pay raise). We told him the missing paperwork for his bonus was found. That's thanks to a retired guy who is running the recruiter station who didn't mind getting in some people's faces! Now we just have to get it mailed into the right place and wait for the wheels to turn. JB told us to please hand his money over to his cousin Kit for investments because if he comes back and there is $20,000 in his checking account he might go out and buy, say... a recording studio or something! (Trust me, the money will be moved!)

Blessings,
Maggie

Email from Maggie dated July 4, 2002

Hi JJ,

JB just called again — twice in one weekend! Bob had prayed Friday night that we would hear from him this weekend :-)

He mentioned this time that the box you sent was especially good because of the homemade cookies, EZ Cheez, and M&M's. I said, "I thought chocolate would melt?" He said the insides melt but not the outside so when they cool off again they are as good as new. But the Skittles I sent (thinking, of course, that hey, it's not chocolate) did melt and melded into one gigantic Skittle bar — not a pretty sight!

Here are a few animal stories from him today that I thought your kids would like:

Apparently the giant lizards there are getting more aggressive. One of them chased a soldier! He said it was a funny thing to see a soldier running from a four-foot lizard. One time a lizard was stuck in their camp and couldn't find its way out. It was hissing at everyone. A guy threw a glass of water on its head, and apparently that was the best thing that ever happened to it! It practically began purring it was so happy.

Once when JB was rinsing his mouth out with water, a trio of birds collected in his spit and began excitedly bathing.

Blessings,

Maggie

Hello Everyone,

Yeah! JB called early this morning! He sounded great and it was a very clear connection. He was at Camp Doha for the day. He'd tried to call last night, but after waiting in the phone line for 2½ hours and then calling Dover AFB he got no answer. Umm, turns out he'd memorized their number one digit off. (Good thing, he was concerned that no one was answering the phones there!)

He's spent the last two weeks almost entirely in the field doing a variety of training exercises, which he assured us he's written us letters about, which maybe we'll receive someday.

He has been to Kuwait City on two different occasions for a day's R and R. Instead of buying gold, he bought $10 Game Boy games and $3 DVDs. (Gotta keep that black market thriving, I guess.) And, of all things, he bought a case of Cuban cigars, which he is shipping home and wants me to wrap in Saran Wrap. (!?!) I'm not sure if this is meant to be an investment or if he's trying to take after his Uncle Bill and El Rushbo. Or maybe it's a statement of some sort. One never knows with JB...but I digress.

Good news tent side: they now have electricity and — ta-da! — air conditioning! He said Kabal NJ is becoming more like a real camp rather than just of a bunch of tents in the desert. One of the main tents even has cable TV. (This is great — they get 150 stations via satellite, but of course only 6 are in English.) And they may be getting Internet access soon. (He may regret having left his laptop with Tyler!)

His tent also has something unique — a large map of South Florida hanging on the "wall." It seems my mother accidentally sent him her map of South Florida in a box of cookies she mailed. Turns out though that about half his tentmates are from Florida so they posted the map and everyone drew circles around where they are from, and it provides a topic of conversation. (Appropriately enough, JB was born in Florida.)

He sends many thanks to those of you who have written and/or sent boxes. It was fun to hear his voice as he described various cookies and other items folks have sent. He said he's received about 1,000 baby wipes but to keep the supply coming. I finally asked him what they are for — I've assumed they are for cleaning his weapons. Nope. Bath in a box. He shares with his tentmates too — and is *very* grateful to be able to do so :-)

He's even received things from people he's never met and finds that great fun. (Thanks JJ and ???) At this time he is not in desperate need of anything but really appreciates cookies, power bars/trail mix, baby wipes, and pictures. Pictures? Yes, he misses home and would love pictures of what's going on in your lives. (Of course, it would be fun to send him pictures of people he doesn't even know — just to keep him guessing.)

JB told us when he goes in the field for long days or weeks of training, he packs power bars, trail mix, and other goodies in his pockets that were designed to carry ammo. I expressed concern that he was choosing snacks over weapons, when he reminded me that he is the driver. "What am I going to do, pop my hatch and start shooting at tanks?" He's aroused the jealousy of fellow soldiers because he purchased a quality thermos that actually keeps water cold. So when everyone else is tanking down the warm/hot water, he pulls out his thermos with matching cup and pours himself a glass of ice-cold water. His sarge asked why the fancy gear and JB replied that he is making the best of a miserable situation. The sarge is now thinking of buying one for himself.

He was excited to hear his motorcycle is fixed and sitting here. It was fun listening to him trying to teach Bob over the phone how to drive it so that Bob could take it out for a spin to keep it running. This is the bike that Bob says looks like it is speeding even when it is in neutral :-) We need Greg Cooper or John Huber over here to go joy riding.

We told him Tyler was returning from the Miami missions trip today, which brought back memories for JB. I also mentioned that as I was driving the kids to the airport for the trip, I'd heard they'd made new rules for this trip based on some of JB's activities in the past. Sigh. Tyler assured me HE wasn't planning on sleeping on the roof of the church. That's all I can think of, except that he still hasn't made it to a Bible study or chapel; he's been in the field so much. Please keep praying for

that fellowship/growth to happen. And thank you all for your continued prayers on JB's behalf. They are much appreciated! Blessings,
Maggie and Bob

P.S. Nicole — JB says to tell you, "Thank you! Finally, a letter from a friend!" Although he had to laugh that you were complaining about the heat wave here. He was calling us in the middle of the day from "one very hot, solid metal box." I asked why there were no windows. "Bullets, maybe?" he said (somewhat sarcastically I thought).

Silers — He sends regrets that he cannot attend Amy's wedding. Although he thought about requesting leave :-) He did appreciate the card.

Letter from JB dated July 16, 2002

Dear Everyone,
I've been having this terrible recurring dream. I'm surrounded by an endless void of sand, dust, and heat. And fools. It's awful. I keep trying to figure out what it means when I awake. When my head clears I realize it's no dream!

That's right, ladies and gentlemen, I, JB Hogan, have really deployed to Kuwait, easily one of the stupidest places for a country in the world.

Why? Well, in the abstract, we are "defending freedom" and "serving the American people," and more realistically perhaps, "keeping allied oil-producing countries aware that they want to stay allied."

But the desert is a distressingly concrete place and you start to see things in a very absolute and fundamental way. Once you reach this way of perceiving things you start to see the humor in spending 50 percent of your time guarding the gate of a kabal that's only there to guard because you're out there to guard it. Also, you grow to loathe anything that even remotely reminds you of a sandbag.

But I can't get too cynical because these past 10 days we've done some pretty worthwhile training. We first had a company-level gunnery. Our crew qualified with a 7/10, which is the minimum, but it was on the first try, so we weren't too upset. We probably would have gotten 100 percent if they had let us know they were changing the ranges on the targets. The briefing told us they were zeroed at 600m but they were really about 800m out. Surprise, surprise, our rounds fell about 200m short. We'll get it during the next gunnery in September.

It's been very hot lately and I've had trouble trying to write during our midday break. I usually fall asleep. And now we've been doing training at night so sleep is precious. But today we have tower guard duty, so I should have plenty of time to make this a long letter and send it off.

It's a good thing we have guard today too. We've jumped back into PT full speed after doing nothing for a while, and I have terrible blisters on both feet. I plan to buy new shoes when we go to Doha on Saturday.

All of your letters have been greatly appreciated. Yesterday I received a box of *Analog* magazines from Reed DePace. They have become pretty popular already. I've even been getting mail from people who are complete strangers to me. This is great! Mom must be passing on my story to a lot of people. However, it also brings up an upsetting irony. Although many of *Mom's* friends have sent me lengthy letters, a whopping zero percent of my friends from home have sent any correspondence to me. These are the people I grew up with — the ones I used cue sticks to sword fight with or teased until they locked themselves in the bathroom (depending on gender). Come on, guys! We used to throw rocks at squirrels together! We used to play Bond until our eyes bled and we were afraid to go around corners without doing a combat roll. We used to try to grill steaks outside without gas in the grill and wound up baking them in the oven while downing gallons of sparkling cider! And you guys can't even jot off a quick note on your computers to me? This is me, seriously considering hiring some new friends. [Editor's Note: In all fairness, I know at least Luke has written to JB.]

Anyway, here is a humorous army story. One aspect of guard duty is the necessity of a quick response force or QRF. This is a squad-sized element, a two and a half ton truck and a driver. It is also more accurately something along the lines of an "Average Paced Response Force," as among others things, QRF is not exempt from the 10 kph kabal speed limit. [Editor's Note: Gotta love the military!] I found this out after I attempted to pick up the trail of an armed intruder. More on that later.

The story continues. It's the final half hour of my shift. Deep in my gut I know that if called, it will always be near the end of your shift. I was, of course, deadly in my accuracy. Two sharp blasts of the horn awaken me from my daydream of reading a thick novel, eating Cinnamon Toast Crunch, and wearing only socks and boxers. I'm by the truck with all my gear ready to roll in under 15 seconds.

The dismounts [Editor's Note: Soldiers who are not drivers] take about two minutes. I utilized this extra time to scratch one of my more entertaining rashes. We finally load up and head out to Tower 4. At 10 kph this was not exactly quick. Upon our arrival the tower guard jumped down and reported he had received visual contact with an armed runner heading towards the AHA.

Okay, the AHA is probably the most sensitive place in the kabal. AHA stands for ammo holding area and exactly 100 percent of our kabal breakout (go to war) ammo is stored there on huge pallets. Now, it is in no danger of being stolen by a running dude as it is all strapped down with metal ties and in huge boxes and such, but it would be spectacularly vulnerable to, say, an incendiary grenade.

But I digress. The scene reverts to the two and a half ton idling by Tower 4. Sergeant Beasley and I are somewhat suspicious of the information we are receiving:

"Which way did he come from?"

"He must have come along this way," said the sergeant at the tower, indicating the supposed direction of travel.

"So, he came from outside the kabal?"

"I guess he must have. We didn't ID him until he was by the tower."

"What? If he came from outside you would have seen him two klicks out. We're in the desert!" This was a good point.

"Well, uhh..."

"Where's the wire breach? Do you see any footprints on that burn over there?"

"Well, he could have breached somewhere else and hugged the burn until he got near the AHA."

"Right. Whatever. Where is he now?"

"We lost sight of him at the AHA."

Great. At this point I didn't know whether to laugh or vomit. We move out. I'm pumped because I still think we are after a real intruder and the tower was just half asleep, hence the shaky setup. Sergeant Beasley recognized it was training at this point. He did seem a little ironic when he got in the cab.

"Let's go!"

"All right! A real target!"

"Vroomm!" (That was the truck.)

"10 kph!"

"Sorry."

We *putter* over to the ammunition depot where an intruder is supposedly already in location. At least the two guards there are still alive, if bored looking.

"Yeah, we've fanned the whole area and there ain't nobody here."

So we fanned it too to make sure. This is the part where I smell a rat because we are all standing around in battle gear waiting for the Bradleys to roll around the AHA, as if they're gonna find him when we couldn't.

And the co's gotta stop by. And the first sergeant. And then we finally leave after an hour with no enemy engaged. Here's the punch line. I complained and griped the whole time about how we were screwing everything up and how it was probably Tower 4's imagination anyway, and it turns out it was a battalion test of the QRF.

Wait, that's not the punch line. The fact that I was awarded a commemorative $^1/_{15}$ INF coin for our QRF being the fastest is! That's all till next time folks.

Wish List:
- Rash cream (clotrimazole)
- Whisk broom
- Ahem, no more baby wipes for the time being. I am adequately supplied, as is the rest of my tent. Thanks to you all for responding so heavily, it is much appreciated!
- Cookies
- Creme Savers are always nice :-)

Next Episode:
Gunnery!
Company Miles Training Event
More Guard Duty!
Adventures in Kuwait City!
Bonus: Near Death Experience [Editor's Note: Sigh.]
And plenty more of your favorite PFC Hogan witticisms!
All this and more next time on: *Help! I'm Trapped in Kuwait!*

Letter from JB dated August 1, 2002

Dear Everybody,

Good (evening, morning, indeterminate insomniac hour). Once again it's time for another fantastic episode of *Help! I'm Trapped in Kuwait!* (Written while on a training exercise living in a Bradley.)

Fade to Black. *Help, I'm Trapped In Kuwait* — Episode IV Starring (so I won't forget): Company Miles Event, Company Live Fire, Near Death Experiences in Kuwait City, and EIB Trainup.

On that note, the TV gag lost the last bit of its (Notice the absence of an apostrophe, kids? Let your parents explain.) novelty and the letter takes on some semblance of structure.

I believe the last time I communicated with you I had explained how I "earned" a Bn coin. That took eight pages to explain and two hours to actually transpire. Coming up is two weeks worth of stuff, which will fit into the same amount of space.

Immediately following the QRF detail, we saddle up our steel horses to participate in a Company Miles event. For those of you who aren't modern military training geeks, Miles is multiple integrated laser engagement system. It's laser tag with a budget. It's extremely expensive and low tech because it was developed in the '80s (like me!) And the prices never dropped. Why should they? Nobody buys it but the military.

But despite all that, it's still kind of neat. It has a laser simulator for the M1A1 Abrams cannon, 50 cal and coax, the Bradley 25 mm chain gun, TOW missile, M16, SAW machine gun, AT4 launcher (kids — that's the bazooka!), and the Dragon (that's a bazooka too, only it's huge and you can actually control its flight!) [Editor's Note: This might as well been written in Swahili. Between the jargon and JB's handwriting.]

The little receptors on your body and vehicle can tell which of these is hitting you and tell you just how dead you are. Armed with that knowledge you should be able to follow this next story.

The Miles exercise consisted of several engagements, many of which I still remember. Our first mission is a straightforward attack on an enemy observation post. Easy, right? Well, it gets real hard when you mis-estimate the range by about 3,000 k! So instead of pulling off a surprise flanking maneuver of the enemy who we thought was just on the other side of this little hill — we surprised and decisively engaged, I dunno, maybe some scorpions or something. Interesting tactical note here: If you flank too early, you give the enemy *your* flank. Think of it as turning a corner in a hallway too soon. You'll notice that you walked into a wall.

The defense was a whole other story. We spent 12 hours working all through that night with the engineers — digging fighting positions, setting up land mines, placing our sectors of fire. But when we were attacked by a battalion size effort, it was a joke: 17 tanks and 9 Bradleys vs. 3 tanks and 7 Bradleys.

Note: 33 percent of our TOW missiles were inoperative. In fact, the best move made by our side was this little exchange I heard over the radio. It was from one of the squad leaders who was supposed to ambush the enemy and then fall back. Upon seeing exactly how much we were being hit by, he immediately ordered: "Don't fire that rocket!! Are you crazy!? They might *see* us! Lay back down, you knucklehead!"

So, most of the dismounts (foot soldiers) lived, thanks to low visibility and a good understanding of firepower ratios.

Considering that before we got rolled up and lost 100 percent of our vehicles, we did knock out nine tanks and five Brads, I think we did okay. This did not, however, make me any less dead.

Letter incomplete. More to follow after this eight-day field problem.

~JB

Dear Friends and Family,

We're leaving for Atlanta today, but JB called this morning (1:30 A.M.) and I wanted to at least get out a short update.

The first thing out of his mouth was, "Mom, do you have any idea how much commotion ya'll have caused here?" He was in the field for training exercises when he was summoned. "Hogan, the colonel wants to see you!" JB said, "I haven't lost anything, Sarge! Here's my weapon and see, here's my Bradley!" The sarge says, "You're in the middle of a congressional investigation."

Turns out our little letter to Senator Carper that Bob walked over to his office last week created a bit of commotion in the desert. The ironic twist? JB received his bonus just before the investigation was launched. But evidently, an investigation, once begun, takes on a life of its own. JB was ordered to go call his parents (thanks, Colonel!) and tell them he'd received the bonus. Then JB "suggested" that we not go back to visit Carper, that, in fact, we shouldn't even wave to him on the street.

JB was having a pretty good laugh over all this. After all, he didn't start anything, and they can't actually get him in any trouble over it. He's got us for scapegoats. But, he was a tad nervous about meeting with his colonel today. Like he says, his goal over there is to lay really low under the radar screen and not be noticed. Which he says he was doing quite well at — until he inadvertently threw this stick of dynamite under the colonel's door.

Thank you for your prayers that he would get his bonus. It's actually just the first $7,000 (tax free!), but that was how it was explained when he enlisted. A little at a time.

Other news — they decided to keep JB as a driver after all; he's now the senior driver and is supposed to look after all the new drivers. He is driving in the lead patrol. He is enjoying it again because he has a new gunner. The gunner stays with him at all times in the Bradley and JB was getting pretty tired of the last guy who was evidently compulsively military in all things. He says the new gunner is so laid back he's "almost a civilian." He didn't get to take the marksmanship test. His weapon remains officially unfired.

They've been told they may come home November 27th. Leave will be arranged in four-day weekends. The guys are seriously protesting this, saying they can't get home and back in a four-day weekend. Please pray they would be reasonable and give the guys a block of time off in December, preferably around Christmas! Hmmm...Maybe I should write Senator Carper...

Anyway, he sounded in great spirits and says other than being under investigation, things are good.

Funny story — his sarge was commenting on JB's incredible supply of baby wipes. JB says, "You know, I told my mom and she mentioned it to everybody and for the next two weeks every box I received had a package of baby wipes." The sarge says, "Why don't you tell your mom you need twenty bucks? You'll go home a rich man." So, how about this: Next time you write, stick a one-dollar bill in it and say I mentioned JB could use a buck!

Thanks for the letters. He mentioned Granddad's, Mellora's, Brandon's, and a few others that he recently received and really enjoyed. Gotta run.

Love,
Maggie

Hey Mom,

Well, they snatched up our phones, but we've got a couple of computers hooked up to the Internet here in the TOC (Tactical Operations Center, thus named so as to seem like we are actually conducting tactical operations instead of cleaning the showers and spreading grease on random Bradley engine parts), and I'm willing to sacrifice some sleep to use it. Also, I have access to a computer that I can just sit down and type on, so a letter should be forthcoming soon. I'll finish it up and email it to you. Also it has allowed me to keep writing a little bit here and there, so as to maintain my sanity. Could you please send my copies of those two stories I was working on?

Well, here's a bit of news. We just got back from the Brigade live fire, which should be our last field problem. Fingers crossed. It was actually kind of neat. We got to see live air burst artillery rounds, and there were rumored to be Apaches lighting up the targets somewhere.

Then the Evil Dust Storm showed up and made us fantastically miserable for two solid days. Ironically I had just turned in my groovy sun, wind, and dust goggles to get replaced. They had a miniscule crack in them and I thought, "Boy, I better get that fixed right away, so they're perfect in case we ever actually get a *real* dust storm around here."

Next in line is the EIB PT test the day after tomorrow and the EIB road march (happy birthday). [Editor's Note: JB's b'day is Saturday.] EIB training should take up most of September. I would be thrilled beyond belief to earn this. It is a very noteworthy award, and it means in the future you don't have to put up with EIB crap when the training comes around. It's mostly memorization, but I fear the hand-grenade event will present a problem, most people who are eliminated are eliminated here. [Editor's Note: I hope he just means from the competition...] A lot of it is luck, and I'm only partially saying that to cover up the fact that I can't throw worth a frog's earlobe. [Editor's Note: Sad, but true. We forgot to teach ball throwing in our homeschool. Who knew?]

Well, this past week (preceding the live fire) has really stunk. At the end of the previous field problem my track's engine exploded. It had been working fine all week, then our new LT, who wanted to see what driving was like, takes over for about 500 meters and the thing shoots out a volcanic eruption of oil from the engine compartment. What was the immediate reaction from the admiring crowd?

"Hogan! What the h—— did you *do?*"

(Hogan pops out of the back of the track, not the driver's hatch.)

"Hey, I was asleep!" (Sometimes that's a fantastic defense, except for say, explaining why you forgot to answer the radio on guard shift.)

Then everyone notices the LT get out of the hatch. The mood...shifts.

"Boy that track was about due for a problem."

"Could be any number of things."

"Let's look for the leak. It must be one of the gaskets for the radiator — those things are *always* violently exploding."

So anyway, we get towed back, and my track is down for a week. One day replacing the part, which means pulling the entire engine out on a crane (turns out it was a bad power take-off unit, which is safely beyond my maintenance level), about 20 minutes to put the engine back in, seven spine-chilling seconds where the crane operator CLANG! slams the radiator against the inside of the engine compartment, and another six days waiting on a new radiator.

So, this puts me and my gunner on rear detachment. Basically we do all the tasks that the company is assigned while they are gone. With 8 people instead of 100. Two on 24-hour duty, two sleeping 24-hour duty off, and the rest to pull KP, police call for the...well...the desert, get ice, take out the monstrous loads of trash that the last platoon with trash duty thoughtfully left for us, and miscellaneous junk. It was miserable.

Also for some reason rear D didn't stop when they got back. The company got time to recover and chill for the next mission while we did their work for them. Then when my track gets fixed, I'm expected to jump right off rear D into the next field mission without missing a beat. They got minimal performance from this driver for quite a while.

So anyway, we're back now, and I'm not stuck with any junk that I know of. So I'll get another letter out to you shortly.

Birthday List:
- Game Boy Advance: Tactics Ogre and Broken Sword. (Amazon.com?)
- More G.K. Chesterton and C.S. Lewis books.
- Gift certificate to Earl Teate Music? Or better, Musician's Friend online? If possible? Aren't question marks great? They can turn a statement into a question?

So, talk to you all later.

~JB

Hello again,

Today has been fantastically dreadful. This morning at 0200 we began the EIB 12-mile road march. The ruck was only about 40 pounds but it seemed to feed off my tiredness as the march progressed and increase in size and mass.

The course was all on asphalt too. My sole had been worn so thin from the first three months here that I could feel every pebble and stone through the boot. The road march started out fine... I wound up next to the new guy in our platoon, a PFC Shelatz and talked and joked with him for about three miles. Unfortunately, I didn't realize that this was slowing my pace down. I was already ten minutes behind pace in only three miles. The rest of the march I spent alternating running for 30 seconds to a minute, then walking twice that time.

By the time I got to the one-mile track for the victory lap, I literally couldn't run any farther.

Then they started calling out how much time until they closed the gate, and then I could suddenly run again. I made it with four to five minutes to spare. I have never hurt this bad on a road march before, not even in basic. The boots, the asphalt, the joking around for three miles, the running to catch up, the not being in shape, they all really add up!

Today most everyone is recovering. A few people got royally taken advantage of and are out setting up a live-fire range. I don't know how, none of us can walk. I hobbled over here to use the computers and let you guys know how I was doing, but I'm really not looking forward to the hobble back.

Tonight I'll probably try to get back on and write you about Kuwait, and maybe finish that funny story. Later.

~JB

Howdy,

Yes, I received the package you sent for my birthday, I'm looking forward to playing with it. Right now all the cool people are out doing land nav, which thanks to a fabulous snafu they have me on record as passed, qualifying expert on their weapons, which by similar snafu they have me down for. All this is of course related to the EIB or for you lazy civilian types the Expert Infantry Badge. Not Excellence in Broadcasting, or Eating in Bed, or even Every Item Botched, my proposed new army motto.

Guess what else they have me down as qualified for? Combat lifesaver. I never attended this course. They have me confused with either Howle (a sound alike problem) or Driscoll (a look alike problem, although both of us vigorously deny it). This means I can stick people with IVs. According to army paperwork anyway.

You're still gonna have to wait on the Kuwait City stories and such. There is a time limit on the Internet access computers now, and the dude with the one I can sit down and chill on is gone for a few days. It's coming, I promise. Right now I'm using this time to check out websites of publishers from that magazine you sent me. Until next time! ~JB

Dear Mom,

Well, I've got the computer right now, and all the leadership is gone out to the ranges or the land nav site, so instead of working I'm going to write a letter. And it is a beautiful thing. The main thrust of this letter is finishing the story that I left off in the middle of, and the adventures in Kuwait City.

Story: So we're inside the Bradley watching the gate, making sure it doesn't run away or whatever, and we've got the radios on the battalion net so we can listen to the shenanigans. Shenanigan Number One went something like this.

"Dragon X-ray this is Tower 2."

"Tower 2, X-ray" (Dragon X-ray is the battalion radio watch. He sounded bored.)

"Roger." (On the radio you say "roger" instead of "uh" or "um.") "We've got a light moving out here...over."

"I copy a light. Moving. Over."

"Yeah, roger. It looks like a chem light or something. Over."

" Does it appear dangerous? Over."

"Roger, negative." (Note: "Roger, negative," although in moron language simply means "uh, no," in proper radio protocol means "yes, no."

"Well, just keep an eye on it Tower 2. Out."

Thirty minutes pass.

"Dragon X-ray, this is Tower 2."

"Dragon X-ray."

"Roger, we've still got eyes on that light."

"Roger. I've identified the source of the light. Over."

"Great."

"It is a nomad herding a bunch of sheep. He's moving about a few feet per, uh..." Long pause. "Few feet per... minute." (Note: A few feet per minute would be so slow as to be unobservable to the naked eye at that distance.)

"That fast, huh?"

"Roger. He's moving pretty good. Over." (You could sense the eyes rolling.)

"Make sure he doesn't try to sneak in with all those sheep. Dragon X-ray out."

"Do you know why I pulled you over?"

"Is it still moving? Over."

"Roger. Over."

"Has it changed speed? Over."

"Negative. Over."

"Has it changed direction? Color or shape? Anything?"

"Uh, that's a negative. Over."

"So you called me to tell me that nothing has changed. This is Dragon X-ray out."

Maybe 10 minutes later.

"Dragon X-ray, this is Tower 2."

"What?" Protocol is inverse to frustration on the radio.

"Roger, I've identified the source of the light. Over."

"Great."

"It's a nomad herding a bunch of sheep. He's moving about a few feet per, uh…" Long pause, "Few feet per… minute." (Note: A few feet per minute would be so slow as to be unobservable to the naked eye at that distance.)

"That fast, huh?"

"Roger. He's moving pretty good. Over." (You could sense the eyes rolling.)

"Make sure he doesn't try to sneak in with all those sheep. Dragon X-ray out."

Now that Tower 2 had a mission and some guidance he stopped about the sheep. He knew what to do now. His job was to keep the dangerous light and the sheep out! We thought we'd heard the last of Tower 2. Stupid us.

"Dragon X-ray, this is Tower 2."

"Hi Tower 2."

"Yeah, I've got a Black Hawk. Over."

"You've got a Black Hawk. As in, you are in control of the situation. He stopped by your tower to ask permission to leave. You're checking his trip ticket right now. Or is he just flying overhead? Over."

"Uh… He's uh… just flying over."

"Aha. That's good. Keep an eye on him. Okay? Make sure those Black Hawks check with us before leaving. Make sure they go through the front gate, okay? *Or* actually don't call a Black Hawk over the radio. If you see a Hind-V or T-80 you can call. Out."

We got to go to Kuwait City as well. This is the closest to death I have come on this deployment. I have been around Dragons and AT4s being fired, two TOW missiles, hundreds of 25mm rounds and countless 5.56 bullets. I sleep on the sand with the scorpions, snakes, and spiders. The other day I jumped up to talk to the gunner right when he started traversing the turret. I've fallen off the Brad six or seven times, and the worst I received was a sprained ankle. I was almost killed crossing a busy street while on R and R.

It was the very first street out of the parking lot. All 150 of us moved en masse to the sidewalk and waited for an opening. When the group started moving, I moved with them. Then in unison they all stopped to let a white SUV go past. I kept walking. It was like in the movies when they ask for a volunteer to step forward and everyone takes one step back. It was total deer in headlights. Time slowed, and my legs stopped responding.

At the last minute I jumped forward. The headlight brushed against my back leg, but I was unscathed. Other than that, Kuwait City was pretty cool. You can buy Cuban cigars there, and electronics are extremely cheap. There are a million jewelry stores all lined up one after the other, all identical. There really isn't a lot to tell. It's a consumer city full of knick-knack and clothing shops. But it beats the heck out of my tent.

As far as what's going on right now, we're still working on training for our EIB trainup, so we can be ready for EIB training. By test day we'll probably be so bogged down with EIB we won't be able to pass any of the events.

Not really. Most of these events are muscle memory and memorization. This is easy for me. They don't seem to understand that I can learn faster than some of the other guys around here, so I wind up wasting a lot of time going back over the events I already have down.

For example, the M16 functions. We'll all be in one tent

practicing the M16 event. You have a total of 30 seconds to load, clear a malfunction, and unload the weapon. At first this was hard. The fastest time was like 28 seconds. Then we started practicing.

Once I had it down I moved to the back of the tent and watched. After a half hour or so they noticed me.

"What, you think you're special or something, Hogan?"

"I've got this task down, Corporal."

"Come over here and prove it. I haven't seen you go yet."

I executed the task in 14 seconds. Because they might look stupid, they managed to come up with a criticism anyway.

"You do it that fast and the grader might not see that you did every step and they'll give you a no-go."

"Roger, I'll make sure I take my time when I do it for real."

"Yeah, just because you can do it fast doesn't mean that you've got it down."

"Corporal, how could I do it this fast if I didn't have it down?"

"At ease!"

But despite the prevalence of NCOisms and time wasted on the easiest of tasks, I still feel confident that I'll get the EIB. Because I never want to do a road march like that again. (Army guys can laugh now.)

That's about all that's going on. Just an interesting side note before I close. Concerning the word *at*. *At* is by far the most dangled preposition at all here. Never will you hear, "Where is the (item)?" It's always, "Where is that (item) at?"

I've tried to explain that the locator is contained in the *is* part of the sentence but it doesn't sink in. Then I tried telling people to police up their prepositions, they're dangling everywhere but they just looked at me blankly.

I've even heard this exact exchange on the radios.

"I need you to find Sergeant Dennis."

"Roger. Where is he located at?"

So in my last ditch effort to try to show how stupid this sounds, I've begun answering questions in the form they are asked. Example:

"Hogan, where are you at?" (Say it out loud a few times. Don't you sound ridiculous?)

"I'm at in the tent, Sergeant."

"Where is Foster at?"

"He's at walking to the chow tent."

They'll never get it though.

That's all for now.

~JB

Email from JB dated September 4, 2002

Hey Mom,

How is everything? Still here in the desert. Yep. Still looking at lots of sand, etc. We had an interesting issue yesterday. At the estimate range to target station, do you get to retest if a herd of camels crosses in front of the target while you're looking at it in the binos? They'll be arguing over that one for a while.

Also it's amazing how easy it is to make really stupid mistakes on simple tasks if you're thinking about other things — like cheese, going home, and so forth. I gotta watch out for that.

Otherwise if I just keep my head on, and my arms and legs attached, and my torso from leaking, I should make this thing. It'd be nice to no longer walk around with no awards on my uniform.

~JB

Hi All,

This is really cool. Getting emails from JB means I don't have to type them myself. Better yet, I don't have to try to decipher his handwriting! This is just an update on the practice tests he's been doing the past few weeks. The real tests begin tomorrow. He has to get a "go" on all 36 stations of the test in order to pass. (Or something like that...) His email follows.

Blessings,
Maggie

Dear Mom,

Another day, another... thing that happens every day. I dunno. How about another day, another packet of Gatorade powder converted into drink and consumed. That's kind of cumbersome. Oh well.

I was doing fantastic today up until I got to the Dragon station. The Dragon is an old piece of junk missile launcher. It's like a baby TOW that one guy can carry around. It kicked my butt. I had to retry about five times until I finally got it right. I got it right the first time three days ago.

So trainup is finished. There is one free day where we can go to whatever sites we want to. I finished with a grand total of five stations with "no-gos," including the SAW, which defeated me twice because I stepped into line to test and left about 60 IQ points back on the bench; the 50 cal, which defeated me the same way; and the FO's station (an FO is a forward observer for artillery, you civilian weenies), which would have been no problem if I had been allowed to complete training on it the first week. Excerpt from conversation:

"You need to move on to the next station now."

"I'm not comfortable with this one. Heck, I can't get this one thing down and I didn't even get a chance to try the other thing."

"We need for everyone to get good training today, and the next group is here."

"I haven't gotten good training yet. I'm still failing every time I pick up this compass. Why don't you graders stay a little late today until everybody is ready?"

"Graders don't stay late."

So I failed the first time I tested. Once I figured out it was just math, really fast, I got it though. As long as I don't drop the binos while measuring my points. (That last sentence was more for my own benefit because ya'll have no idea what I'm talking about.)

And then the Dragon. I don't know what happened there. The sight wouldn't lock into place. I can picture it falling off in combat. (The missile goes wherever the sight happens to be looking...)

But anyway, I've got all these things down now, and I'll go over them again tomorrow. And since I passed hand grenades first time twice in a row, it means it's about time for a fluke double no-go. I mean, I should be fine... one of the two.

That's the gist!

BTW — I don't need any more individually wrapped baby wipes. I've got over a thousand! The army started supplying them too. The Lewis Grizzard book was fabulous. I'm going to be a columnist. I can finish things if they aren't supposed to be over two pages. [Editor's Note: ADD runs in my family!]

And if you write a hundred two-page essays, you've got a book! It's all so simple now. [Editor's Note: Right.]

That's all for now.

~JB

P.S. Tell everyone to keep writing emails — it's neat to hear from total strangers who know my life's story!

Email from JB dated September 6, 2002

Howdy.

Why don't you take the step up to the next level and learn how to use AIM? Come on, Mom, you've got this email thing down, it's time to expand. Tyler, your 15-year old son, can teach you. He's only half your age, and he can do it just fine. Well less than half, really.

So anyway, training for the day is finished so I am diddling around on the computers for twenty minutes at a time adding all kinds of things to my Amazon wish list. It's exciting to me. It's also frightening how fast I could cause all this great money I've earned to vanish. But some of these items are necessities, so I'll just have to come up with a long-term plan. Maybe as long as a month! I'm confident I'll earn my EIB now. I'm hoping to get all first-time gos now. This is called going "True Blue," and it earns you an ARCOM, which is like an AAM on steroids. It's actually a noteworthy award; many people go their entire first enlistment without receiving one. Unless they are pogues who go to Germany where they give them out to crews who shoot distinguished. The driver gets one too. How stupid is that? A driver gets an ARCOM for knowing that "driver up" means forward and "driver back" means the other way. In real units all you get is an AAM. I didn't even get my AAM because my gunner was a first timer and didn't nail the troops with the coax. But there is another gunnery on September 17, and I am confident we'll shoot distinguished this time. The more decorations on the uniform the better!

Talk to you later.

~JB

Hi All,

JB called this morning to wish Tyler happy birthday (and you Jim and you Kit!) and to catch us up on his EIB testing — 36 testing stations over 3 days. You can fail (no-gos) two stations and still pass. Three fails and you drop out. Friday was the first testing day. He'd wanted to buy an EIB patch to have in his hands as a tangible reminder of what he was trying to do — a way to remind himself to concentrate. Unfortunately, he couldn't get one. Then a box from us arrived in his mail call with crackers, Cheez Whiz, and a Sam's-size stick (log!) of pepperoni.

JB said, "E-I-B-pep-per-ron-e. Okay — this is my lucky pepperoni!" And put it in his cargo pocket (Of course, half of it stuck out!)

Last week JB got a no-go on one of his tests. This morning he made a mistake on the first test of the last day and received his second no-go. The rest of the day, at every pass, he took another bite of his EIB pepperoni in celebration. He watched as his buddies dropped with their third no-go, one at a time.

The last test comes — the one he'd had trouble with last week and asked for, but received no, help on. He had to use binoculars and who knows what else to figure out how large and how far away a target was — some sort of math thing. Anyway, the wind was fierce and he couldn't hold the binoculars as still as he would have liked. He first wrote down 350 km, then debated with himself. (JB has always held to his first answer on tests, saying when he changes an answer it turns out wrong.) Was it really that large an object? If not, his distance would be off. The sarge began the countdown in seconds:

Five, four, three. On two, JB scratches out 350 and writes in 315. Sarge looks at his paper. "What's that number?" (Okay, handwriting is not a strong suit around here.) JB says, "315, Sir." Sarge says, "Good thing you changed that number, Son. Pass."

So I told him, "Lots of people have been praying that you'd do your best."

JB said, "Thanks! And I was one of them!"

JB is on cloud nine. Thank you for your prayers. He needed some encouragement and this was it! He was the only one in his squadron to make it. They have an awards ceremony on Wednesday.

~Maggie

Hi All,

Well, I stand corrected. In case you are interested, here is the corrected version of the email I sent out recently. I knew I should have just waited for JB to write it :-)

The good news — yes, he passed. The bad news? I am lousy at details! My comments have the silly little email arrows in front of them, followed by JB's corrections (or comments as the case may be) :-)

~Maggie

> >EIB — *testing 36 stations over 3 days.*

JB's comments: Not to mention the death march around Doha, the land nav course, which thankfully I did back in Benning, although it still stunk to have to work 20-hour days for three days. Plus I had to shoot expert, but that was recreation, not work, as far as I was concerned. Thirty-six stations sounds like a lot, but some of the stations are things like: put batteries in device. Clip device to weapon. You are a go at this time :)

> > *You can fail (no-gos) two stations and still pass. Three fails and you drop out.*

JB's comments: Of course, you can also fail the same station twice in a row and get out that way too. So when you make your first mistake, you don't really feel like you've got the leeway that two more chances affords you.

>> *Friday was the first testing day. He'd wanted to buy an* EIB *patch to have in his hands as a tangible reminder of what he was trying to do — a way to remind himself to concentrate. Unfortunately, he couldn't get one. Then a box from us arrived in his mail call with crackers, Cheez Whiz, and a Sam's-size stick (log!) of pepperoni. JB said: "E-I-B-pep-per-ron-e. Okay, this is my lucky pepperoni!"*

JB's comments: By the second day, people were referring to it as the expert infantry pepperoni.

>> *Last week JB got a no-go on one of his tests. This morning he made a mistake on the first test of the last day and received his second no-go.*

JB's comments: Yeah, and it didn't help that what I did was so unbelievably half-witted. Okay, 50 cal rounds are supposed to load one way. You can *physically* get them to feed backwards, and the first one will even fire, but only if you are a persistent type, willing to pull the charging handle about fifty times. The irony? I set one of the speed records for the 50 cal during trainup. The other irony? I stared at the round for like five minutes before I started. I knew something was wrong with the way I was holding them, but then I followed the old army maxim, "Don't doubt yourself! Your training will take over; just execute!" I certainly executed myself on that one.

>> *The rest of the day, at every pass, he took another bite of his* EIB *pepperoni in celebration. He watched as his buddies dropped with their third no-go, one a time. The last test comes — the one he'd had trouble with last week and asked for, but received no, help on.*

JB's comments: No. This is not true. It was one of the absolute easiest ones during training. They just so happened to move all the targets around, and one of them in particular was tough. Because when you're doing math with small numbers, the variance between multiplying by one and by two is huge. On big numbers multiplying by 80 and 79 isn't that big a difference. Darn exponential variation!

>> *He had to use binoculars and who knows what else.*

JB's comments: Just binoculars...

>> *Anyway, the wind was fierce and he couldn't hold the binoculars as still as he would have liked.*

JB's comments: or at all, even.

>> *He first wrote down 350 km.*

JB's comments: Note to those of you scared to death of the metric system who probably didn't know this: Even with the most advanced optics in the army, I couldn't spot a target 350 km out. However, 350 m was within the range of my binos...

>> *Sarge looks at his paper. "What's that number?" (Okay, handwriting is not a strong suit around here.) JB says, "315, Sir."*

JB's comments: JB has only called an enlisted soldier "sir" once in his army career and regretted it so thoroughly that he has never done it again. JB said, "315, Sergeant." Military types will understand.

>> *JB is on cloud nine. Thank you for your prayers. He needed some encouragement and this was it! He was the only one in his squadron to make it.*

JB's comments: JB is not in the air force and, as such, has not been allowed to be a part of a squadron.

Email from JB dated September 24, 2002

Howdy,

We have returned and life has gone right back to its old unpleasantness. I don't even remember all that is so unpleasant, except that there is no longer a routine. The EIB weeks were great because we did our work at the same time every day, finished off when we were done and were left alone afterwards. Plus, the ready access to computers was nice. I just hate it here, never knowing when you'll have to suddenly break out of your chill out and go perform some bull that could have been done during the day. Oh well. One more month, if I don't flip out before then. Or maybe it's two months, I don't even really know.

Don't really have anything to update you with and I have no humorous anecdotes with which to entertain you. I poured out a couple pages of creative energy into a dialogue about how difficult it is to write dialogue and my reservoirs are currently tapped.

Although my correspondence will be less frequent now, as there is exactly one (I counted twice) computer for our whole company, please continue to write. I will read and respond when possible. This goes for you too, my slacker friends.

Actually, I can't call all my friends slackers anymore. Lauren is living and working in Baltimore now. That's impressive to me. And frightening. I guess it means that my friends and I are moving solidly into the young professional set, the set that actually has to check for wedding rings on that cute waitress and discusses what a terrible day they had at the office (or in my case the ditch or the tent or the driver's hatch... ugh...). You know, the set of people that start getting married left and right.

Oh, where have the halcyon days of my youth gone? It seems like only a breath ago that I was young and carefree, with a wide world of expansive opportunity. Before I wax too nostalgic I should remind myself that I was also lazy and evil and worthless, and had a misogynistic chip [Editor's note: Yup.] on my shoulder the size of a...big...thing...Yeah. (Don't let any editors near that sentence; it is surviving in a quantum state of literary uncertainty. If I go back and observe it, I fear it'll disappear.)

Let us move on forthwith. I yearn for a spell checker on this machine. [Editor's Note: I did ya'll a big favor!] Also a 3.5" diskette drive which would enable me to extract the story I wrote on this other computer next to me and send it on to where it can be appreciated, nay lauded, by all who receive it. [Editor's Note: Hmm... Doesn't that make two computers? And JB says I can't do math.]

Oh well. I'm going to hit send before I strain myself trying to come up with more pedantic verbiage. (Bonus: Look up *pedan-tic* to see why it's my new favorite word!)

~JB

Maggie's Postscript: Ya'll do me a favor. Next time you write JB, use a word or two that will stump him. He only has a Scrabble dictionary there (no definitions!) so this should be fun! Also, he is interested in cookies again ;-) as well as the following.

- sardines
- Vienna sausages
- any sort of canned or preserved meat
- and individually wrapped granola and stuff for taking in the field

---

Email from JB dated September 27, 2002

Hey Mom,
So anyway. The past couple of days I have been taking a CLS class. This stands for combat lifesaver and basically means: "Well, we figure you're not good enough to be an actual medic with like morphine and responsibility to make life and death decisions, but we will let you carry around this little bag with gauze and some aspirin."

Today was the last day of training. It centered on qualifying with an IV. Not only did I have to receive an IV, I had to actually stick someone. No big deal, right? Only I hate needles with a passion so intense that I lose consciousness within minutes after skin breakage, whether it's a tiny 20-gauge IV, a shoulder shot, or a blood test. Doesn't matter. [Editor's Note: This is the absolute truth. Seen it.]

And I had to watch my arm while I received the needle. Yeah, rough tough infantryman and all that garbage, but show me a needle wrapped in a medical package and I go to pieces. Little pieces. To complicate matters my veins are deep under the surface and my blood pressure is so low that they don't inflate — even with the constriction band. Not even the medic was able to successfully stick me. So, I guess I'm glad I didn't have to deal with the bleeding everywhere thing, but it still stinks to have them fish when your vein rolls out of the way.

Ironically, my first partner had the same problem with his veins. Although you could see them because his skin was, like, translucent, the veins rolled all over the place. I couldn't get a bead on him. I felt bad because I really messed up his arm looking for them.

So, they gave each of us new partners with big veins to stick, and we were able to get it. I goofed up on the removal phase though. I was concentrating so hard on pulling it out fast to avoid hurting him that I forgot to hold a piece of cloth on him and put pressure on the entry site. I just yanked that bad boy out. He jumped at least a foot. The medic couldn't stop laughing. I didn't think it was funny. But he made it, and the liter of blood he lost was balanced out by the IV saline I had just given him. Him never talking to me again was an unexpected side effect. Oh well.

Tomorrow is the big test. The head medic asked me if I was nervous. I asked if it was multiple choice. He said yes, so I said I was completely confident. He asked if I had been studying, because it's (gasp) all of 80 questions. I said no. If it's multiple choice, I said, I can beat the test. He didn't really like my attitude, but I didn't like his haircut, so I felt we were about on even terms.

So what's going on at the home front? It sounds like we'll still be coming home. Going back may be a whole different story, but I don't have any information that CNN hasn't given me so I'm still just guessing.

Talk to you later.

~JB

Hi All,

Had a phone call from JB yesterday. He was just checking in to let us know he's fine. He's been out in the field a good bit but said, "Unfortunately, absolutely nothing funny or even of interest happened there to report."

Praise the Lord!

He is dreaming of coming home, seeing friends and family, and sleeping on a mattress. They are hearing that it will probably be December...

He did pass the exam for combat lifesaver but fervently hopes he never has to give anyone an IV.

Blessings,

Maggie

Dear All,

JB called yesterday morning and also dropped off a quick email. His big news is that they seem to be actually coming home! December 5 is the date being used right now, with possible leave over Christmas! That would be the best Christmas present Bob and I could hope for. (Departure is almost two months away so he would still appreciate your prayers and cards.)

~ Maggie

Email from JB dated October 16, 2002

Hey Mom,

Not much time, really. Just a few things, so you have them written down: motorcycle, call Benning, investments (spend my money!), airline tickets, look at something for December 21! Don't buy yet of course.

Only one remotely funny army-ism today. I don't even really feel like writing it right now for fear of not doing it justice, but I promised you something. Before second BDE comes in, we have to get our pad "all ready" for them to take over. This consists of throwing away all the tables and shelves that we carefully built from scrounged wood. These things made our lives drastically more bearable in our tents. Bookshelves for our gear, tables for the cards (and later TVs), and shelves that went over our cots to hold all our snacks and stuff. All gone. At great effort to us.

Also, the rubber mats we laid down across the sand to the shower things were all removed. These were crucial to showering because otherwise on the walk back you kicked up a bunch of dust and were no longer clean. We removed them. Things we replaced and fixed at great effort? The sandbag borders around the tents, which supposedly create visually appealing pathways etc., but in fact had no significance whatsoever. They were referred to as the Martha Stewart bags. These, of course, had to be perfect and new for second BDE. I'm sure they'll be thrilled to hear of our labors for them...

~JB

Hi All,

JB called this morning and then sent this email. He said he'd been assigned to move vehicles at Camp Doha for the last several weeks. Once he arrived there he found a line of about 50 big trucks and heavy equipment. The drivers were all told to pick out a vehicle they were licensed to drive and then jump in. JB, ironically, though a "driver" is not licensed to drive anything! So he jumped in something he thought he could handle and drove. He had fun driving all kinds of different vehicles for a few weeks.

He's excited about all the investments his cousin Kit has made on his behalf. He's now putting money into stocks instead of Game Boy games :-)

He picked up a training manual for the aviation test one needs to take to be allowed to apply to warrant officer school. He is very interested in pursuing the goal of becoming a helicopter pilot. I think my cousins Speir and/or George did this in Vietnam??? (If so, let me know guys. JB would love to pick your

"Astute, dude!"

brains!) Anyway, it was good to hear him talk of goals instead of complaining about how dumb everything is :-)

Blessings,

Maggie

📎 Email from JB dated October 30, 2002

Hey Mom,

I'm back in the kabal again. Unfortunately, someone stole my cot while I was on this driving detail. It's kind of irritating. It's not so much that I use it, I sleep in an empty tent now on the floor because that way I can turn out the lights and sleep when I feel like it rather than when the least tired soldier does, but it's the principle of the thing. At least I hadn't signed for it.

During the week or so before I left for this driver's detail, we had established a word of the day program. Each morning I'd

...During the week or so before I left for this driver's detail, we had established a word of the day program. Each morning I'd come up with a word and everybody would learn what it meant and try to use it as often as possible during that day. Wednesday's word was astute.

I was having trouble getting the meaning across. I said it meant insightful or observant but it obviously wasn't getting the right connotation in their minds. So I said, "If you say, that statement was astute, it's the same as saying that statement was right on." A brief pause, then someone said, "So it means right on!"

"Yeah."

"As in like astute dude..."

come up with a word and everybody would learn what it meant and try to use it as often as possible during that day. Wednesday's word was *astute*.

I was having trouble getting the meaning across. I said it meant *insightful* or *observant* but it obviously wasn't getting the right connotation in their minds. So I said, "If you say, that statement was astute, it's the same as saying that statement was right on." A brief pause, then someone said, "So it means right on?"

"Yeah."

"As in like astute dude!"

At that point I had lost control of the crowd. High fives and cries of "astute dude!" And "aw astute man!" filled the tent. It stayed the word of the day and pretty much the rest of the week, just not the way I intended it.

~JB

Email from Maggie dated November 17, 2002

Hey JB,

I'm off to Nashville with our book proposal in hand. Pray!

You won't believe this: guess what you received in the mail yesterday? A letter from West Point inviting you to apply based on your ASVAB score. It says every year about 150 regular army soldiers are offered admission to the U.S. Military Academy. Sixty percent of their evaluation is based on academic performance!

Just so you know. Do you want me to send back the card requesting an application?

Yes! A thousand times over yes! Please reply to them as quickly as possible! Is there a website? Phone number? Send two copies of the letter! That would be fantastic.

This is probably a little late, but I'm praying about the book proposal. Of course, I've read a study that chronology is irrelevant in prayer and the events prayed for. Of course, that raises the question, can we pray that the Indians don't lose all their land to the Europeans? How about praying the Romans adopt Christianity before Constantine? Or better yet, how about we get everybody to pray that the snake gets stepped on by an elephant on the way to the woman. That'd be great!

Anyway. I just read *The Mouse That Roared* and the *Mouse That Saved the West*. Really fantastic books. I recommend Leonard Wibberley to everyone. Only you can't find his books anywhere. Anyway, for once we got off at an almost reasonable hour today, hence the letter. Things may start picking up. I'm also slightly less apathetic about everything army since hearing about that letter, so maybe things can go better. Tomorrow we're working with civilians anyway and the chain of command should be nowhere in sight. Yeah!

~JB

Hi All!

We are so grateful to the Lord that JB is back from Kuwait and home on leave! Thanks to everyone for their many prayers and words of encouragement these last six months!

JB leaves Sunday afternoon to head back to Ft. Benning. He'll be there until his unit is re-deployed to Kuwait — if it is.

You're invited to:

A drop-in for JB (a welcome home and a send-off all in one) on Friday night from 6:30 – 8:30 P.M. No need to bring anything but your family. Stop by on your way out shopping or to other events. He'd love a chance to see you.

If you know you are coming, drop me an email. If you don't and find later you can stop by, please do so!

~Maggie and Bob Hogan

Email from JB dated December 10, 2002

Hi All,

I'm writing this from Dover, Delaware! I have successfully completed my deployment to Kuwait. That means coming back with all the salient parts still attached and all five of my senses still operational. There was some brief worry that my sense of smell would never return, thanks to endless dust storms forcing upwards of a pound per week of dirt into my nostrils, but I think I picked the last Kuwaiti-dirt-containing booger out of my nose about an hour ago. It was kind of an emotionally fulfilling moment.

This is the last in the critically acclaimed "Help, I'm Stuck in the Desert!" series, and it is with a twinge (albeit a very tiny one) of regret that I close this chapter in my life. However, even now I see that the next series is titled, "Help, Even Though I Finished the Desert Part, It's Not Like I'm Out of the Army or Anything!" There will be a sneak preview at the end of this letter.

But the point of writing this was not simply to amuse myself, although I try to work that into anything I do. The point of this dispatch is to thank everyone for the fantastic home-front support I received during this deployment.

As daft as the army motto is right now, I did feel like an "Army of One" out there. I had an entire supply unit, an intel gathering team, and MWR service just for me. The packages were all greatly lauded by myself and my tentmates who knew there was no way I was eating all 900 of the cookies I'd receive that month. And baby wipes... near the end there we almost dreaded seeing baby wipes!

All the stories and letters you sent did wonders for distracting me from the rigors of desert life. Twenty minutes of bliss goes a long way toward maintaining mental health. Even those of you who forgot to put your name or a return address anywhere on the package or letter had wonderful things to say about what was going on in your lives, and someday I hope to figure out which one of you bought that new classic car you were so excited about!

Leave is about halfway finished. Unfortunately, due to the political situation, I will most likely not be able to come home for Christmas. Please continue to keep us in your prayers since we are preparing to re-deploy (not definite yet!). If we do it'll be the real thing this time.

~JB Hogan

P.S. Sneak preview of "Help I'm Stuck in the Army!"
This could happen. Today we washed the floor. It wasn't dirty. In fact, it was the floor of a locked room that most people didn't even know existed, and the floor was covered in plastic. But we ripped the plastic up and cleaned underneath, and somehow it was still substandard and had to be redone. I think the dirt we brought in on our bodies was more than the dirt in the room, and that's what the inspectors saw. But it only took five hours to get this room back to the level of cleanliness that existed before we showed up, so I consider it a productive day. You'll never believe what happened next...

Thrills!

Spills!

Details!

Join our hero in his continued battle to pit sanity against bureaucracy, and lose every time!

Laugh!

Giggle!

Groan in useless sympathy!

See our hero: Whine about not getting promoted while he makes fun of his leaders! Complain that 200 years of tradition doesn't mean it makes sense to (fill in army task). Lock his door and pretend he doesn't live in a barracks with 200 other slightly witless individuals. You'll read these serials' content in the knowledge that *none of this is happening to you*!

Hi All,

We had a wonderful visit with JB here at home. He really enjoyed his friends and family. The two weeks were over all too quickly.

He called the other night to say he has received re-deployment orders for January. Back to the desert. Right now he has no phone and no email. If you have a chance to drop him a line over the next few weeks, he'd loved to hear from you.

Thanks for all your prayers for JB over the past year or so. Please keep it up. And it's a great time to remind us each to remember all our military personnel right now, especially those who will be celebrating Christmas on foreign soil.

May the light of Christ illuminate your Christmas.

~Maggie

Email from Maggie dated January 02, 2003

Dear Friends,

Most of you know, or have guessed, that JB will be deployed soon. Well, it's official. He heads out in two weeks.

Most of all, please continue to keep him and our other military personnel in your prayers.

~Maggie Hogan

Commission spares historic buildings from demolition

By JEFF BROWN
Staff Writer

Two 19th century homes on South State Street have been spared a date with the wrecking ball under a plan reviewed Thursday afternoon, Jan. 16, by the city's Historic District Commission. The commission also considered a request for the construction of a new, three-story office building behind the houses.

The commission's decision resolved a crisis that had developed during its Dec. 19 meeting. During that session, the five-member panel was asked to consider the complete demolition of the two homes as well as the partial demolition of a third structure. That building, commonly called the Gambrel Roofed House, dates to around 1760, and is thought to be one of Dover's oldest buildings.

Historic preservationists decried the plan, saying it would eliminate a valuable reminder of Dover's working class neighborhoods and forever change the face of Dover's traditional southern gateway. Members of the commission itself expressed reservations about the proposal, and voted to table it until they could obtain more information about the properties.

Acting City Planner Dawn Melson said early Thursday that developer Mike Zimmerman had turned in a revised plan that called only for the partial demolition of the two homes. As with plans intended for the Gambrel Roofed House, only the more modern portions of the old buildings were to be removed, Melson said.

Former Supreme Court Justice Henry Horsey, a champion of historic preservation in the city of Dover, argued against construction of the new office building as well as the original demolition plan.

Ultimately, the Historic District Commission gave the plan its blessing. By a split vote of 3 – 2, it sent the plan for the office building to the Dover City Planning Commission. In a separate motion, the commission also recommended approval of the plan for partial demolition of the three homes on South State Street.

DEPLOYED

Déjà Vu...

Dear Mom and Dad,

I've arrived here safely, although I'll probably have talked to you on the phone before you receive this. Mail here is only collected once a week and unless I can figure out what days it is collected for other pads, my letters will be somewhat significantly delayed. Send some stamps if I haven't told you already they are much quicker than free mail. Your mail should get to me at about the same speed as last time. Try it and see!

Things I may need while I'm thinking about it. (Note: Anything sent in a box larger than a shoebox will be returned to sender.) Another set of those goggles. I decided I need a tinted set to go with my clear set. Dare I ask? Baby wipes.

I finally got Sarah's letter. Let her know it showed up the day before I left. It was pretty neat; she didn't use an envelope. Instead she folded up a map into the shape of an envelope and taped it. Can you get her address? I'd like to write to her.

Okay, I'm sure you are all curious about the living conditions, so here goes:

- Cramped.
- Odorous.

There are tons of people on this kabal now. Every single pad that was here before has had huge chow tents set up around it, and they are all filled with soldiers. I believe additional pads have also been constructed. These white chow tents are everywhere too. We have a chow complex now, with an on-site kitchen. That means better food but enormous lines and waits.

There is also a shower and water shortage. We are showering every three to four days out here. Gruesome. And it doesn't help that there are like 60 people in each of these big tents. We've started a twice a day PT (physical training) schedule too. Those of you who can make the connection here will understand why these two things together are so much worse than their component parts would suggest.

Okay. On that note, on to things that are better this time around:

- Our vehicles are in very good shape. Although mine drives like a cow, it happens to be a fast cow. As long as I don't need to turn very often things should be great. [Editor's Note: How reassuring.] Maintenance should go well this time because we have a lot more mechanics, so maybe we'll be able to really keep these vehicles running.

- We have a regular training schedule as well. It is, of course, all secret and stuff. Heaven forbid the Iraqis somehow find out which exact battle drill Bravo $^1/_{15}$ is working on Tuesday, or I would tell you all about it. I could probably enclose a copy of the schedule because they are so swamped with mail handling I'm sure they don't read our outgoing mail. They told us they monitor the phones for operational security. I don't buy it. But I'm also nowhere near stupid enough to test it out.

- Another thing that is better is the MWR facilities. There are two tents with AT&T phones set up. Although this is nowhere near enough to handle the volume of soldiers' daily calls home, it is nice that we even have them. They are much more reliable than the DNS phones and the wait isn't completely ridiculous.

- There's a barbershop, so I won't be getting rid of all my hair and looking like an imbecile for the rest of the deployment.

I received another award today. I earned my driver's badge for tracked vehicles for having completed one year as a driver with no accidents. It's a little early, but, hey, I deserve it. It's an award you can wear on your Class As too, although they only come in Sta-Brite, which means I have to buy a 35-dollar set of buttons and new marksmanship badges to wear it. I'm sure that means nothing to all of you and some of you probably only processed the part about being out 35 bucks but let me tell you, woe is me. I have vigorously stood against Sta-Brite as long as I could. The medals look like cheap plastic!

The flight out here wasn't too horrible. It was an MD-10. Or were they called DCs when this one was made? I can't remember. All McDonnell-Douglas planes are MDs now, so maybe that title functions retroactively.

But the point is, it sucked compared to the Boeing 757. Boeing rocks. The flight went quickly though; I was able to sleep a lot. We stopped in Shannon again and milled around for a bit, and we also stopped somewhere in Italy but were forbidden to leave the plane. That was the worst three hours of the flight. It was no less comfortable than the actual flying but mentally it was deeply distressing. No reason was given as to why we had to stay on.

We arrived in Doha and got off the buses at the all too familiar Lot 5. This is where "turn in" took place last time and also where I had all of my motivation surgically removed. We jumped right into vehicle draw, and I quickly discovered that my vehicle was in perfect condition, except the intercom didn't work. This was possibly an even bigger problem than the nonfunctioning hood of last deployment. (See "Adventures in Kuwait" episode one.) In fact, it was infinitely worse. The hood would have been a real hassle in the field, but the track could still move, shoot, and run over retreating enemy soldiers without a care in the world. Now a field problem would go something like this:

Commander: Okay driver, follow those guys.

Driver: (Contented staring)

Commander: Follow them!

Driver: (Onsetting boredom)

Commander: Hey! Can you hear me?

Driver: (Lays seat back and attempts to catch a quick nap)

Commander: (Vigorous cursing)

Sound of driver's hatch being opened from outside.

Commander: WAKE UP!

Driver: (Groggily) I wasn't sleeping... (You are required by the army to say this after being woken up.)

Commander: FOLLOW THEM!

Driver: Roger.

Vehicle follows.

Commander: Okay, don't hit that wall.

Driver: (Silence)

Commander: Don't hit the wall!

Driver: (Is busy tying bootlace)

Commander: Stop!

Commander: Stop!!

Commander: STOP!!!

Commander: ST-

Wall: THUD. (That's wall for "stop.")

Driver: (To himself) Geez, didn't he see the wall?

Commander: (Giving up on driver) Gunner pick up a 12 o'clock to 3 o'clock scan.

Gunner: (Contented staring)

Commander: Gunner.

Gunner: (Happy tuneless whistling)

Commander: Gunner!

Boot connecting with helmet: Thud!

Gunner: Huh? What?

Commander: Never mind. Just pay attention, we gotta move again. Driver!

Driver: (Contented staring)

Etcetera.

So the communication thing is a bit of a thorn in my side. However, after a Kuwaiti national and his yard boss hopped (I'm using the term lightly now; the dude was way too huge to hop anywhere) into my track and fidgeted with everything except what I told them was causing the problem (they wisely saved this item for last), they eventually brought my intercom back to some semblance of functionality. This lasted nearly three days before it started weakening and fading again. But I'm getting ahead of myself.

Major problems solved — it was time to get to the kabals! The Bradleys, in the interest of fuel conservation and preventing unnecessary wear and tear on the tracks, were loaded onto flatbeds (which we call HETs for fear of unintentionally communicating clearly) for delivery to the kabal. Drivers rode with their Bradley in the cab of the flatbed. Everyone else piled into the bus and followed behind us. Or so we thought.

We arrived outside the kabal at around 11:00 that night. I anxiously awaited my squad leader to appear and guide me off the vehicle. And waited... and grew sleepy. Just before I seriously considered going into low power standby mode, a random person jumped onto the HET and started giving me arm signals to back off the vehicle.

Irrelevant side note, it really is totally unnecessary to guide someone off the flatbed. All you need to do to get off is to put the Bradley in reverse, floor the gas, and remember not to steer. An emotionally unstable chimpanzee could pull it off. Although, perversely, a human with no thumbs and an IQ of 210 could not...

Anyway. As I alluded before, the bus did not travel with us. For some reason it was important that B $^1/_{15}$ show up at the same time that our engineers, C $^3/_{17}$, did. So we went up to the kabal and parked. Then waited.

My heater doesn't work.

The temperature dropped to around 32 degrees. Did I mention my heater's lack of functionality? It got to the point where when another driver knocked on my hatch to ask what was going on, I told him I didn't know but he should feel free to hop in my hatch with me. He was thrilled, as the 10-foot journey from his hatch to mine had sucked all the warmth from his body.

Eventually (read daybreak) the engineers showed and our leadership made an appearance and we all went to the kabal and parked.

Since then not much has happened that I can really write about. We are not allowed to discuss our training itinerary, subject matter, or quality thereof, but I will describe it to you as "somewhat stupid."

Although there have been a couple of days here I actually enjoyed. (Don't tell anybody.)

News is making its way to our ears. We've been hearing about the discovered warheads bit, and the part where Saddam said no army would survive Baghdad, and we assumed he must have been talking about his when we move in.

More to follow when anything that is both interesting and unclassified happens. Don't think my knowledge of classified information is cool however; you would not believe the kind of garbage the army will classify.

~JB

Email from JB dated January 22, 2003

JB writes:
And now, another fantastic snippet of literature from your favorite (unless of course you have your own personal son in the military) desert-livin', opinion-givin', poet laureate of Bravo $^1/_{15}$ Infantry.

Good evening everyone. I have no idea how this letter is going to turn out or even if I'm going to get it done anytime soon. I have a million things to say, but 576,942 of them are related to training events and I'm not allowed to talk about them. About 3,256 of them (this is a rough estimate with a $^+/_-$ of about 3 things) are rants and I really don't need to mail any of my depression home. It's festering just fine over here in the tent.

In fact yesterday a huge angst monster festered into existence and moped around the tent for an hour asking for a back rub and some morphine. Neither were offered but I let it have half of my M&M cookie. It didn't eat it. He just kind of stared at it and cried.

Anyway. We've still got 419,802 things to say. Let's estimate that I've forgotten exactly half of them now that I'm actually typing on my little box. So I've got 209,901 left. I would say of that number, 187,551 of them require an excessive amount of army lingo. I'm really trying to not do that so much. I've calculated that I lose a milliliter of my soul every time I spout an unexplained acronym or army program, and I've decided that if I don't stop soon I'll wind up turning into a vampire.

So we're down to 22,350. One of the things I wanted to mention is that I've been listening to *Motorcade of Generosity* by Cake a lot these past two days and it has done marvels for my sanity. I heartily recommend it to everyone except Ralph Nader, Cary Yules, and Satan. Ralph Nader spooks me, Cary won't return my phone calls, and Satan and I aren't on speaking terms anymore. [Editor's Note: I don't know who Cake or Cary Yules are and I hope I'm not going to regret not editing this paragraph.]

And anyway! I'm down to 22,349. I'm going to have to skip over about 19,563 of these out of consideration for my laptop's battery life, which is sadly not a groovy sodium lithium long life battery but instead is... the other kind.

So, 2,642 left. Now it's getting tricky. I don't have any really good excuses for eliminating these. But some of you only scanned that last sentence because you are such huge geeks that you've actually been double-checking my math and noticed the subtraction error in the last calculation.

Out of disgust I'm going to just cut out all of my remaining topics and bring the number down to two. Which is what I'd been planning on doing all along.

First off, I want to deeply thank all of you who were so incredibly generous to write me those long emails. I was barely able to read them all in one of my nightly timed sessions. Next time I go to the computers I'm bringing a disk with me so I can save them and re-read them at my own leisure.

(The word *leisure* is used loosely here.)

But in all seriousness, keep the words flowing my way. Even if absolutely nothing interesting has happened to you in weeks (a state of being I long for), I guarantee I'll deeply enjoy reading about it.

I really wish I could respond to you individually at this point but I'm not going to be able to pull that one off until I download your little pearls of news onto my own computer. Plus, I am faced with an existential dilemma; it has been so traditional for me to email home these great open letters to everyone that I feel like I'm stealing from the content of my own series if I write anyone individually. But the thing that'll actually decide whether I write individual letters will be free time.

Free time is at a premium here. We have added daily night training (that didn't sound right) every day except for Sunday. Every day is a workday. A long workday. We should be really busy here pretty soon too, doing... stuff. So you'll be getting nothing, and you'll like it! Aren't army phrases stupid?

Unconnected fragment: on Sundays we don't shave in order to conserve water. It's the only thing I've really been thrilled about out here.

I've been playing with my video camera too. I've got some interesting footage and I think it'll give you guys a great idea of what things really look like out here. However florid my language is you'll never really be able to picture a 60-man tent in the middle of Kuwait until you see this one. Also, I've got a few skits planned, and as soon as we get a chance I've got a few guys who want to help me film them.

And the final thing I have to tell you:

It poured down rain last night! Naturally our tent leaks and everyone who sleeps against a wall got all their clothes and personal items soaked. It was horrible, but I was secretly very pleased that I'm in the middle. I'm not good at sympathy, and I couldn't have any empathy because it didn't happen to me so I went back to listening to my CD player.

The rain had a side benefit for us though, although I didn't notice it until much later. It was terribly cold today and I had to guard a tower. The wind picked up about an hour into my shift and howled the entire remaining five hours. It was miserable. But I realized the rain had packed down the dirt and removed all the dust, so there was no sand storm — and that one would have been a doozy! So really not only was the rain no misfortune for me, I actually profited from it. No one else seemed to be amused by this observation.

I promised myself I wouldn't do any specific complaining in this letter, and I don't plan to. I can't really think about specific things right now anyway, and besides we have established a tradition of ranting about everything that we hate during the three-klick walk to the chow hall, which really helps. Besides, there's always the next letter. Stay tuned!

~JB

And this letter starts right back up because I have been on guard duty again and unable to get to the Internet to send it home. Not much has happened since yesterday when I wrote the last bit. But there was something I intended to talk about and I would alternate back and forth between remembering what it was and being excited about it and then forgetting what it was and being very irritable because of it.

Unfortunately, right now I am smack in the middle of the forgetting-what-it-was cycle. Well, perhaps I will blather a bit about other things until I remember what it was. I can start with mentioning a few things I could use now. Did I tell you that the shoebox thing was no longer in effect? Just keep in mind I don't have a need for large non-perishable items...

I could use some additional batteries. [Editor's Note: Guessing he means AA size.] Not like a trillion of them but a couple of dozen would more than suffice. I could use some soap cases. The PX seems to be perennially sold out of them. Gum. I like gum.

I've been playing around with my video camera a bit more too. I've got some good video of soldiers goofing around and the lines of vehicles outside. Next time I walk to the computer tents I'm going to film the whole thing so you guys can get the idea of how long it is.

I'm really starting to believe that the thing I was all excited about telling you isn't going to sidle back into my consciousness.

So here's a funny story about me causing problems. They have toasters in the chow halls, but they aren't the pop-up kind. They're the cafeteria style where you lay the toast on a little conveyor and it comes out the other side.

So, I've gotten into the habit of taking Kraft Singles and laying them on the toast so I can make hot cheese, bacon, and egg sandwiches in the morning. Well, last night they had gourmet night. We got steak (medium rare and everything!) *and* shrimp and they had a little salad bar and there was mozzarella cheese and bacon. So I helped myself to a bowlful and was planning on making a fantastic sandwich.

All truly great sandwiches are toasted.

So I piled up my bread with cheese and bacon and laid it on the toaster. About three seconds too late I realized that the toaster had a very low ceiling. All of my piled up bacon and cheese was neatly scraped off the toast and fell down into the heating filaments, promptly bursting into shooting flames.

I casually sauntered away with my cheeseless toast just as the panicking Kuwaiti came running toward the toaster. He viciously unplugged it and began frantically saying to no one in particular, "No toaster! No toaster!"

Many were clearly confused because this flew in the face of the facts, as there was, obviously, a toaster.

~JB

Email from JB dated January 28, 2003

Hi All,

This just in from Kuwait:

Although there is very limited time here on these computers and they are obviously depressed, as evidenced by their inexplicable sluggishness, I will still attempt to be humorous in the letter.

First things first. It has been quite hectic here lately. I have a new job now; I am the colonel's Bradley driver. No, it is not a promotion, it is a lateral transfer. Same job, more important guy. [Editor's Note: Here's hoping the colonel's Bradley is in the *back* of the line should they go rolling off to war!] Although because I'm so close to the paperwork guys, my promotion will be expedited possibly in the next couple of months, depending on how many slots they receive.

I have had to move all of my stuff and settle in and do some field stuff with my new track and haven't had an opportunity to get on my laptop and write out a real letter home. One is forthcoming. I also got some neat footage of some tanks firing out at the range today. They said boom, but it wasn't so much what they said, it was the *way* they said it.

More to follow...

~JB

Dear Mom, Dad, and Extended Fan Base,
Greetings once again from Kuwait, the land of a thousand horrors. Well, really there has only been one horror, but it was pretty gruesome. It poured down rain last night. I remember often thinking to myself the last time I was here that the only thing that redeemed this place at all was that it was never bone chillingly cold and rainy. I really don't get it. This place is out to get us.

Yesterday was the first opportunity I've had to do some laundry since I've been out here, and I was thrilled. I had absolutely no clean clothes left so it was just in the nick of time. I hung them out to dry, which this time around isn't an instant process like it was during the summer. They hung all morning and afternoon, and I checked them after dark and they were still mildly damp. So I decide I'd go pull my last guard shift and gather them up wet or dry after that.

Enter the downpour.

Thankfully I wasn't on tower guard this time around; I was the ready response force not to be confused with the quick response force or even the lethargic response force. So I was inside my hatch, which leaks but only in predetermined areas, which I have memorized. I was for the most part able to contort myself around the drip areas, although in my sleep I let my left knee get thoroughly soaked.

However, my laundry wasn't so lucky. The only thing I can say is that the weather did a thorough job of rinsing them for me. If they ever dry I feel pretty confident that they will be clean.

Microsoft Word has just informed me that I write on a seventh grade reading level. So any children you have under this age shall not read my letters unless they can pass a final exam in seventh grade English and literature. If a child's head explodes, don't say I didn't warn you.

Hopefully Mom spell checks some of these before they make it to you because I forgot to on a couple of them and that last paragraph will sound really idiotic given the gross misspellings of words like *sandwich* and even *foot*.

Right. The above bit was all written and compiled on the 23rd. It is now *exactly* the 30th. My laundry is still wet. Much has changed and I even have in my actual mind right now exactly which stories I had planned to write home about. I'm going to write them out right now before I forget, because I am likely to be in the middle of writing one and the other one will sneak out of my nostrils and run chortling off into the desert.

So here they are:

I went to Doha Port and it stunk.

I am now the LTC's Bradley driver. The way I was selected is mildly humorous.

Oh, you want elaboration? Well you, my dear reader (or if this is being read to you out loud — my favored readee), you are in some kind of luck because elaboration is what I do! I sincerely hope that your email server supports italics and underlining because I'm in an emphasizing mood!

Okay first story. The punch line really is rather short and I could probably sum up the whole spiel in a paragraph, although you would totally miss out on the *horrible dragging boredom* that was interwoven in every waking moment on this detail. So I'll try to drag it out in my own inimitable way.

(Ego shield holding at 110 percent.)

First, let me begin with a brief explanation of what exactly we were doing over there. There were about 60 – 70 of us selected, based on — ostensibly — what kind of vehicles we were licensed to drive.

For those civilians out there let me explain why this is a joke. People select which vehicle they actually drive not based on what their license says they can drive but rather on what I call the "Dude! Let me drive that bad boy right there! I ain't never seen the inside o' one o' them!" factor, commonly referred to as DLMDTBBRTIANSTIOOOT.

But anyway.

We were arranged into tracked vehicle drivers, wheeled vehicle drivers, and TCs. A TC is a dude who rides in the turret or command seat of any vehicle. For convoy purposes you don't need one if you are taking a wheeled vehicle; it's just like driving a car or large truck on the highway. But track vehicles usually have drivers in really bad places (except the Abrams — everything is cool about the Abrams). The idea is it's important to have somebody up high on the track who can see all around the vehicle and say things like "don't hit that bump on the right," and "try not to kill any more small children, okay?"

So the army, in its infinite wisdom, has made it mandatory to have a TC in a tracked vehicle when it's tooling around populated areas. This is a good idea.

However, since we follow the letter of the law and never the spirit, we have a driver and TC in the vehicle and they both wear Kevlar helmets. There is absolutely no possible way for them to communicate. But the law is appeased, both soldiers have hard head covering and there is a driver and TC in the vehicle.

If, however, the TC wanted to say something critical to the driver, the only possible way would be to climb down out of the turret, struggle through the squad compartment, worm their way through the passageway connecting the driver's hatch to the squad area, and whack him on the back of the head with the ball peen hammer. By this time the message has gone from "watch out for the hole!" to "I really wish you hadn't slammed into that hole."

I told you I could elaborate. I haven't even technically started the story yet!

I may have to make this a two-part letter because I'm getting leery of spending this much time blatantly not working.

Back to the beginning — 60–70 people selected over a period of three days to drive vehicles. About 15 were designated tracked vehicle drivers. There were a few miscellaneous truck drivers and the last 40 were all to drive Humvees. I'm sorry, HMMWVs, as is the proper army nomenclature.

We were given a packing list that changed approximately three minutes before chow, and naturally I was having trouble getting ready in time to eat. I was told that if I had to miss chow so be it. I let my team leader know firmly that I wasn't planning on missing chow, and he could interpret that as he saw fit. I was told that I should have been ready last night. I mentioned that this information would have been welcome to me last night when I had plenty of time. I was told that everyone else knew but me, so it must be somehow my fault. (This was later proven to be a total fabrication on his part; he was too lazy to tell anyone.) I said whether or not other people knew a piece of information had absolutely no bearing on whether or not I knew it, and it was his job to tell me.

This led to a blazing row and a counseling statement, but when he saw me give up on pen and paper for my entry in the "I Disagree with This Counseling" section and begin typing my response and occasionally checking my dictionary, he quietly got rid of the statement due to the personal embarrassment it would have afforded him. He said that that was my warning, and I told him he was a worthless leader. It pretty much petered out after that.

[Editor's Note: As much as I want to comment on the preceding two paragraphs I will restrain myself. But I must admit I somewhat sympathize with the team leader, even if it was his fault...]

Blast! Sidetracked again! Back to the story.

We were all ready and packed to go. Our items to carry included an assault pack (heavy), a cot (awkward), a sleeping roll (bulky), an NBC pack (excessive), a flak vest, a Kevlar helmet, and an ammo vest (stupid). This was a lot of stuff to have to carry all in one trip, so naturally they decided the best place for the buses to pick us up would be at the top of the hill. It gets better later though...

Naturally everyone was somewhat excited about this detail. It was in Doha after all — showers, batteries, baby wipes, and buildings to sleep in. Wrong!

We were going to Doha Port. Not Doha — Doha *Port*! It's like Doha's annoying uncle who only shows up uninvited and looking for free room and board. And he smells like white zinfandel and cream mints. (I don't actually have an uncle like this; I've just heard about them.)

We got to stay in, surprise, a giant chow tent exactly like the one we were already staying in, only with no lights. Yeah!

I'm going to have to hold off on this story and finish it tomorrow. It's late and I have duty from 1200–0600.

More to follow...

~JB

Email from JB dated February 8, 2003

Dear Home,

I left off in the middle of the Doha Port epic last letter so I will try to pick up exactly there:

We're in these giant chow tents just like back in the kabal. No access to a px just like in the kabal. No showers available to us just like in the kabal. But, unlike the kabal, there are no lights in the tent. So it kind of stunk.

But the mood was still hopeful as we were away from the company main body — even though we comprised more than 50 percent of B Company's strength. If we were under Doha Port authority, or even Transport Command authority perhaps we'd be utilized efficiently. We were in for a surprise. [Editor's Note: Are you surprised?]

The recent attacks on the U.S. civilians, as well as a few shots fired at convoys had thrown the system into disarray. Suddenly, civilian HET trucks (that stands for big honkin' truck) could no longer transport tracked vehicles to the kabals, despite MP escorts.

Also, somehow, someway, 50 percent of our Humvees had been misplaced. Yeah, figure that one out. We found some in the Marine's corrals and the rest scattered all over the units: infantry, support, and artillery, all kinds of places.

My favorite were the Marines, though. They, of course, buy into the whole "Sir! The best of the best of the best! Sir!" pile of dragonfly kidneys thing, so we intended to have a little fun with them.

We approached their corral, and of course it was guarded by a couple of lance-corporals. (Army corrals were only sporadically fenced, let alone guarded.)

Us: Hey, we need to look at your vehicles.

Jarheads: What do you think you're doing here?

Us: Hey, do you guys actually have rounds or are you pretending to guard?

Turtle 1: (Uncomfortable silence)

Turtle 2: You can't just come in here.

Us: Hey, that Humvee says TB043. I can see it from here.

Turtle 2: So?

Us: That's one of ours; explain to me why you have it.

Jarheads: You'll have to talk to higher. (Stepping away from gate)

They had like four of our vehicles. Most of them were not remotely surprised to see that they had vehicles belonging to another unit. Especially ours.

Artillery guy: Yeah we heard about you guys.

Me: What? You're from Fort Carson!

Artillery guy: Nevertheless...

I left it at that.

But that was an ongoing task, and not in chronological sequence of the part of the story we are currently in. Just assume as you read the rest of this that at any given time there are at least two hapless guys wandering around the three square mile area looking for lost Humvees. We began to wonder if our vehicles would sneak out to other corrals at night to get away from us. It was getting creepy.

Back to the tent. We didn't realize that two or three command levels above us the situation was in absolute disarray. The last thing we had heard was that if you were assigned to a particular vehicle, and finished driving all the ones we were assigned back to the kabal, you got to stay there and chill until everyone else got back.

The rumor mill immediately began cranking out speculation on top of theory about which vehicles would run out first. After the hubbub died down I smugly pointed out that there were like 50 Humvee drivers and only 1 (me) M2A2 driver. Someone offered that there were probably three of them and I'd have to make multiple trips. I said they probably only assigned one driver because there was only one of them, which was how it turned out.

For those of you who have good memories, you'll be wondering why in the last letter I stated that there were 17 track drivers.

This is true. Five of them were for 577s. And the other Bradley drivers were assigned to slightly different Bradleys, BFSTs, and Linebackers, which are artillery spotter vehicles and air defense artillery respectively. They are both Bradley hulls and turrets but with different electronics and seating configurations. The Linebacker has four stinger missiles instead of a TOW. [Editor's Note: Wake me when the technical stuff is over...]

In theory, if I had driven my one Bradley back and they still had more BFSTs or whatever, I should have been called back to help with those, but I knew the army's ability to shut off rational thought and look at only what is in the paperwork. I was confident that I'd be safe behind my red tape bunker.

Not that it wound up mattering in the long run...

Back to the short run. This is where the story breaks down a little and a whole lot of time passes but very little occurs. We were basically put on standby to drive our assigned vehicles whenever they called us up. The first night they came in and woke everybody up at around 0200. [Editor's Note: For us nonmilitary type people, this would be 2:00 A.M., which back in the old days was when JB was wide awake!] We were told the entire convoy was here. We were only to grab our helmets — no weapons, no gas masks, nothing. We formed up outside the tent.

Note: This is about a 70-man formation, so it's like 6 rows of 12 people all standing outside, bleary, incoherent, and wishing a thousand atrocities upon the heads of whoever woke us up. We receive our briefing (none of which anybody was in a mental state to comprehend), and we were filed out to stand by the vehicles.

Key word here is filed. Instead of marching the formation like an intelligent human being (I can't believe I'm saying this, usu-ally I hate being marched when we could all just walk there like normal people), we are filed out row by row. This means the train of people stretches practically from our start point to our desti-nation! This was only a sample of what the experience was going to be like...

Ominous Portent 1:

We line up and stand there. And stand there. And stand there.

Ominous Portent 1 Alpha:

While we are standing there, we notice our platoon sergeant, who is in charge of this whole shindig, get bored and wander off.

Finally, someone with enough rank that we hope they might know what is going on comes by. Before we can even ask he says, "I don't know what is going on so don't ask." He walks away.

Finally good old SFC Dennis returns. He has the scoop, so to speak. Apparently we weren't actually needed for anything, but he did happen to notice some other group that could use a hand. So he takes the first couple of rows and sends them off vaguely to the left. I never see them again...

The rest of us are told to continue standing by and he walks off again. I decided that it's about time to downgrade from standing by to "sitting by," and within five minutes of my bold flaunting of procedure the whole formation is in various positions of recline. I feel like I have a purpose again. [Editor's Note: He hasn't changed as much as I'd like to think.]

But the feeling is short lived. After being briefly yelled at for sitting down in the middle of a vehicle staging area, while at (and here I must stress that the word *technically* applies in the fullest) the position of at ease no less, we are told that it is time to get on a bus, travel 700 meters in it, and then help bring vehicles off the ship. Cool — a purpose!

However, this bus is apparently not connected to our particular strand of space/time and it took us around an hour and a half to travel said 700 meters. This is where the whole thing gets very weird and Stephen Kingish. We all naturally went into states of fitful sleep while on the bus and passing in and out of consciousness. Play some weird organ music here and make the screen go all swimmy.

When we disembarked we were... back at the tents! Aaaahhh! Any minute I expected to look around and see everyone lurching around like zombies or perhaps be attacked by a bunch of crazed kids a la *Children of the Corn*. I was tripping out.

We began lumbering our way toward the tent, and, as if picked off by snipers, 20 of us were snatched to — get this — go drive vehicles. I'll never know if they actually did or not, because I, in fine army tradition, can vanish into my surrounds at the first hint of being released. [Editor's Note: Too many years of reading Beatle Bailey.]

Sleep.

Here the story breaks down even further. Although this was the bulk of the adventure, I can sum up what we did in two paragraphs or less. Ready? Go!

Every time after that when we were called upon to take vehicles, we would take everything we brought with us. This was around 75 or more pounds of gear, none of it arranged in a way as to make carrying easy. The average trudge to wherever it was we had to go was about a mile. Every single time we got there, we were told to stand by for at least an hour, then told, "Never mind, go on back."

This happened four times.

See? Here is the basic punch line of that entire story: I was selected for a driver detail, gave up three of my days, stayed in a tent with no electricity, and hauled 75 pounds of gear 12 miles to move a total of one, count 'em, one Bradley. And I didn't even drive it most of the way. It was placed on a HET and I slept inside the squad compartment for the actual ride out to the kabal.

There's more story.

Now I'm sure most of you have only trudged through this lengthy diatribe to find out what CD it is that I have been listening to this time, so you can go out and not buy it. Technically, I've still been listening to *Reel Big Fish*, but I am about to put in Buckethead's *Colma*. [Editor's Note: Since I have no idea who these groups are, I am almost loathe to mention them. Do not, I repeat, *do not* go out and buy CDs based on JB's recommendations. Trust me.]

Now, I know what you are all thinking, "Isn't Buckethead that guy who does all his shows and studio appearances with a Michael Myers mask and a KFC bucket over his head? Isn't he the underground deity of shred guitar, with blazing licks so fast as to make Eddie Van Halen take trumpet lessons? Isn't he also the guy with the lunatic obsession with robots, farm animals, kitschy Japanese monster flicks, and sketch comedy set to blazing guitar riffs? The answer is, of course, yes.

But this release is unlike anything I've ever heard from him. Each piece is intricately arranged and many contain full orchestral accompaniment. It's a beautiful piece, with a few songs even taking their cue from traditional Celtic music. I'd even, and I say this about few pieces of music I enjoy, play this for my mom. [Editor's Note: She, however, may choose not to listen.]

And that's all. The tale of my selection as the LTC's driver is coming soon, as well as a brief discussion of the new MREs, and why people in the army will leave you stranded in the desert [Editor's Note: The sounds of that do not warm this editor's heart...] and much, much more.

Well, not much more.

Write!

~JB

📎 Email from JB dated February 10, 2003

Hey Mom,

I am a driver. In fact, that appears to be my calling in the army. I had only been a ground fighter for two weeks when they sucked me up into the mounted trap. Now that I have a year's worth of experience driving, (not quite, but they gave me my driver's badge, which is awarded to you after a year — in theory) I was seriously expecting to get onto the ground and stay there awhile.

However, having a lot of experience as a driver means you run the risk of getting selected by battalion and brigade-level officers to be their drivers. What are the odds for that though, right?

Yeah, right. So here's how the selection process in this case worked. There are two times that people get sent from a line company to headquarters. The most frequent is when headquarters says, "We need one guy." They might possibly even mention what section he'll be in, or on rare occasions they'll say what job they need him for.

February 10, 2003

"There are some pluses and minuses to this job. A plus is that you'll make rank quickly. Who wants to make the next E-grade early?" Obviously we all raise our hands. At least that's what you would assume. Poor PFC Thomson, one of my best friends, and, in all honesty, a total spoon, instead of raising his hand merely stares blankly. After a moment his brain processes that he missed something, and in a brilliant recovery he says, "Huh?"

For those of you who do not know what a spoon is, consider the following expression: "I may not be the sharpest knife in the drawer, but you, Private, are a spoon!"

First Sergeant says, "Step back, genius."

In this case the various line platoons scramble to get one of their guys into the position. The guy selected is — by consensus of his team leader, squad leader, and platoon sergeant — the absolute worst soldier available. This happens frequently to new guys. It's kind of like in Starcraft when you are at the maximum unit limit and you've got an individual space marine with like three health points left so you send him off on his own to attack the enemy base so that he gets killed and you free up resources to create a fresh unit.

Same concept here. The problematic (I'm using nice terms here) soldier is shunted off somewhere where he can't really do much damage, and a slot is opened up in the line to get a new soldier, who will hopefully be an improvement.

Then there is the other case. This is where headquarters specifically asks for a man to fill a position — such as the sergeant major's ratelo, or the colonel's driver. This request is often accompanied by significant glances, or even the demand that the company send more than one candidate for an interview, possibly with the sergeant major.

Response to these is mixed. The platoons know that they have to send a decent soldier, but at the same time they are, of course, reluctant to waste somebody worth their oxygen on Headquarters. Often, if the platoons catch wind that headquarters will be sniffing around for somebody, they'll make sure key personnel are on a detail or in the field at the time, hoping to stick another platoon with the loss.

In this particular instance, most of these games were eliminated by our first sergeant (1SG) since he called for every single driver to be interviewed all at once.

The interview was humorous. Here's what happened: we

were all lined up in numerical order of the tracks that we drive. First Sergeant Seboya went down the line and had us introduce ourselves to him. Then he began asking specific questions. First candidate was E-nothing (an army expression for a PVT, E-I, which is represented on the uniform by a blank space as opposed to stripes or chevrons, etc.) Hall.

"How long you been in Hall?"

"About a year, First Sergeant." (I wish so thoroughly that I could be doing these voices for you right now! First Sergeant Seboya is friendly, but a very direct man, and Hall is a wormy little guy with a backwoods drawl.)

"Why don't you have any rank, Hall?!"

"I lost my rank first, Sergeant."

"Lost it? You mean you had it pinned on, but it fell off in the sand and you couldn't find it?"

"No, First Sergeant. I got an Article 15." (Standard paperwork used for punishing enlisted soldiers.)

"Aha. What for, Hall?"

"Smoking marijuana, First Sergeant."

"Okay, well go ahead and take a step back, Hall."

(Muffled laughter.)

First sergeant cannot send someone with any kind of paperwork issues, promotion flag, or pending disciplinary actions. I see him remember this halfway through his next question.

"Keaton, how long have... Armstrong go ahead and take a step back."

No one else knows why this happened, but those of us from first platoon know this is because Armstrong is likely on his way out of the army because of his inability to keep his weight on the correct side of the army standards. More muffled laughter.

"Whoa!"

"Like I was saying, Keaton, how long have you been in the army?"

"Three and a half years." Pause. "First Sergeant." Keaton is not a huge fan of military custom and courtesy.

"And how long do you have left on your enlistment?"

"4 months, 3 weeks, 2 days, and 17 hours. "

"Judging from the pinpoint accuracy of your answer, I assume you are not re-enlisting."

(Blank stare) Any sentence with *re-enlisting* in it fails to register in Keaton's mind.

"Alright. Take a step back."

"Calderon!" Calderon looks like either a 250-year-old goblin, or a Muppet. It depends on the light. Calderon looks up and First Sergeant Seboya is hit with the full force of Calderon's visage. He jumps visibly.

"Never mind. Step back, Igor— I mean Calderon. Okay, bring it in guys." The group gathers around him.

"There are some pluses and minuses to this job. A plus is that you'll make rank quickly. Who wants to make the next E-grade early?" Obviously we all raise our hands. At least that's what you would assume. Poor PFC Thomson, one of my best friends and, in all honesty, a total spoon, instead of raising his hand merely stares blankly. After a moment his brain processes that he missed something, and in a brilliant recovery he says, "Huh?"

For those of you who do not know what a spoon is, consider the following expression: "I may not be the sharpest knife in the drawer, but you, Private, are a spoon!"

First Sergeant says, "Step back, genius."

It takes him a moment to realize who the genius is. Reverse psychology and sarcasm have always left him hanging.

"Okay next group question: What is your PT score?" Time to lie! All of us give suitably high numbers, but not so high as they'll make an actual effort to check. We make sure we sound confident and end in numbers like three or seven, and not zero or five so it appears that we have memorized it exactly last time we took the PT test.

The rest of the selection process consisted of general motivation questions like these: Are you confident? Can you do this (fill in inane army task here) well? Can you work unsupervised? (Please! I'd kill to!) Do you want the job?

It was down to two of us, and we were sent off to battalion

to interview and test-drive the Bradley. We both performed equally well in every respect and the final decision came down to uniform.

Mine had an EIB sewn on it.

I knew that thing would eventually come in handy for something! That afternoon I was packing my junk and hauling it over to battalion to start my new job.

And that's the story. More stuff will follow, as soon as I have time to type it. I'm still listening to the same CD, so my musical recommendations have not been updated.

However, I am reading the *greatest* book I've read in a long time. It is called *Cryptonomicon* by Neal Stephenson. It is a fascinating study on information theory and cryptanalysis. It has some very complicated math in it, but is written with such a prosaic voice that it makes it fascinating. Douglas Adams meets Stephen Hawking, with a touch of Chuck Pahlaniuk. It is the first book that I have been thrilled to see was over a thousand pages long just so I can be reading for ages.

It contains two distinct storylines (well, distinct so far, two characters from each time period have the same last name, which I take as a huge hint). One is about an information technology startup company laying fiber optic cable in the Philippines, and one is about a special cryptology detachment during WWII. Every few pages a fascinating idea about information theory or cryptology in everyday life is presented and you have to stare into nothing with the "huh" expression on your face as the implications sink in. I heartily recommend it to anyone who wants to learn tons of new words (I really wish I had my dictionary here; his vocabulary is impressive) and is not offended by sailors who curse like actual sailors and (worse) Marines who curse like Marines. However, even with the military type characters, the profanity is sparser than in say a war movie like *Saving Private Ryan*. Final verdict, if you can see that math has more applications to real life than just keeping yourself from being swindled at a retail outlet and this excites rather than frightens you, read this book.

That is all. Thank you for the prayers, packages, letters, emails, and generally pleasant thoughts that have been emanating from all my friends, family, and total strangers who receive my letters from Mom.

~JB

Hey Mom and Dad,

I just now found out that you didn't receive the last letter. I'll try to get it out tonight or tomorrow. Sorry I didn't do it sooner. I haven't been down to the computers in what seems like forever. It has been busy here. We're hearing more and more of the go to war or go home type stuff, and we're told that we'll do one of those things as soon as we know which one to do. Duh. Interestingly enough go-to-war preparations are remarkably similar to go-home preparations, so it is very difficult to tell which one is likely. Of course, I've been telling everybody lately not to make predictions based on what the *army* is doing for crying out loud. Talk about basing your conclusions on a limited and skewed perspective! Anyway, a letter is coming out soon. Possibly two if I have time between laundry, maintenance, and miscellaneous to write another one.

I'm really glad you guys liked the box. Also, bought myself the *Back to the Future* box set before I left. I had forgotten how timeless (ha! ha!) a story it really is. I plan on watching all those *Star Treks* with you when I get out of this hole. Talk to you later.

~JB

Hi,

Let me start off by saying that I have already attempted to write the next few paragraphs to you twice now. The first time I typed them up I attempted to send them and they vanished into Yahoospace forever. I was miffed. Being the dogged stoic that I am, I immediately began re-typing the letter to you, fingers flying like a swarm of gnats.

Regardless, here is a final reproduction of that ill-fated letter, in as close to the original text as possible:

I got Dad an extremely cool birthday present. It's from Ireland. [Author's Note: See appendix B to find out what this was.] It should be ready and shipped out just in time for his actual birthday. If I am still out here, you have to write me and tell me as soon as you get it. I really want to know what you think. You'll be greatly surprised at the minimum. [Editor's Note: Somehow this makes me a little nervous...]

I also found some really neat heraldic maps of the English Isles. They have England divided by region and colored in with the heraldry of the premier family in that area, and all around the map are names and their family colors. It's very cool. They sell them for about 10 bucks apiece but I got them to send you two for free because I explained that you retail maps and might be interested in wholesaling these if you liked them. At the very least if you don't want to sell them they'll look really groovy in the computer room. [Editor's Note: He knows the way to his mother's heart!]

And that's about it. Without further ado here's the actual letter designed for enjoyment by kids and grownups, ages one to one hundred. Read each word carefully, as it is, in fact, a perfect individual piece, designed for flawlessly complementing an exquisite textual tapestry — and you may never read something so delightfully pleasing to the mind from a modern author again. I plan on writing the reviews on the backs of my own books... [Editor's Note: I do not doubt this one bit.]

MRES!!

Let me tell you about the new MRES. These thrill me to no end! We often define the very flow of time by the passage of these brown-bagged surprises from their extremely flammable cardboard boxes [Editor's Note: How does he know they are extremely flammable?] [Author's Note: Because I've set them on fire numerous times. How else?] to our field-grubby mitts, into our hydrochloric acid powered digestive tract, and finally, into a small hole in the desert and buried.

MRES used to be an enemy. If you weren't one of the first people to snatch one of the few tolerable meals, you were stuck with an appalling concoction — such as the loathed and feared Bean and Rice Burrito, which appears to have a candle wax coating.

But Sopako Packaging Company in their feeble, but heartening attempt to toddle generally in the direction of progress, has begun to rectify some of the more heinous crimes against cuisine. The Bean and Rice Burrito, sadly, still exists, but a token effort to improve it has been made by adding a small packet of picante sauce and replacing the peanut butter with cheese.

Many other meals have been tweaked as well. Spaghetti w/ Meat Sauce has been changed to simply Spaghetti, and now tastes just like a bowl of SpaghettiOs. This is something to dance about! And the new Beef Stew no longer contains huge gelatinous lumps of indigestible animal fat! Joy!

And a new dessert has appeared. It is the long-rumored Dairy Shake. When I was finally able to confirm its existence with my own taste buds, I nearly wept. The potential for MRE chefs to use this is phenomenal — even more so than the Cocoa Beverage Powder — as the dairy shake comes in Strawberry, Chocolate, and Vanilla.

Jeff Anderson, this is especially for you. If only I could see what Frosty [Editor's Note: Frosty was one of his friends from Basic] is doing with these. As astounding as his concoctions were with mere peanut butter, cocoa, and varying amounts of water, I'd love to see what he has done with these. He could probably write his own cookbook by now. [Editor's Note: I hope Jeff's mom can mail this to Jeff in Afghanistan!]

But that is small stuff compared to the leaps and bounds made in other areas. For example, the sadly under-equipped meal, Chicken and Rice (which was always like a second fiddle Jan Brady when compared to the culinary delights contained in the older sister Marcia Chicken w/ Noodles) has finally been removed and replaced with (glory be!) a hamburger! Beef Patty as the meal is called in MRE speak is a triumph of shelf-stable cuisine. It contains two pieces of Wheat Snack Bread,

"You had the burger last week!"

Cheese Spread, and BBQ Sauce, as well as a dessert in the form of a Pound Cake.

Introducing such a fine product was a risk though. There is the real potential for soldiers to lose their lives in scuffles over this meal.

Also, Cappuccino Powder has surfaced in a few meals, replacing the more pedestrian Instant Coffee contained in the accessory packs. And, about half of the Tabasco sauce bottles have been replaced with red pepper packets, and now they also include generic Mrs. Dash in little packages! Yeah!

Stranded in the Desert

Those of you with elephantine memories are perhaps wondering why, in fact, people in the army will leave you stranded in the middle of the desert. [Editor's Note: I do not possess even a mouse-sized memory but believe this is in reference to an earlier email in which JB alluded to being stranded.] The answer is, of course, that they couldn't think of a viable solution so they ignored the problem. Here's the short tale.

I was driving a Bradley toward a staging area. No, scratch that, it was more of a pre-staging area. Only in the army do you have to prep, in order to stage, to assemble — before you can drive all of one mile to the drop-off point.

Regardless, we were all lined up to get ready to go, and my track mysteriously disengages the fuel to the engine, cuts off its own master power, and leaves me with a creepy, haunted feeling. I tried repeatedly to restart the vehicle but to no avail. When the convoy moved out, the track [Editor's Note: Short for Bradley. I think.] behind us simply pulled around and even had the sense to yell things like why aren't you going? and hey, what's wrong with your vehicle? (As if I knew but didn't feel like fixing it to keep from being stranded.) But they didn't have the sense to stop and attempt to render assistance to us.

About three seconds later I reached the point of blissful apathy. Being the highest ranking man on the track, I hurled my Kevlar to the ground and began yelling about the stupidity of fellow soldiers. Another three seconds passed and I reached the state of cold-hearted abandon and began walking toward the nearest set of lights.

The other soldier with me, however, was not so eager to set out towards parts unknown and pleaded with me to try to start the vehicle one last time. I said, "Look, even if there was nothing wrong with the track, I killed the battery just then trying to start it over and over." But he was insistent, so I decided to humor him.

In classic sitcom style it whirred to life effortlessly on the first try, despite the battery meter being fully in the red. My personal vehicle won't even start in the yellow, so this one was obviously mocking me. We proceeded to re-evaluate the technical specifications of the Bradley, specifically in regard to top speed, and were able to catch the convoy.

Lucky for them.

You've been a great audience, thank you and goodnight!

~JB

Little Creek restaurateur says "au revoir" to French wine

By JEFF BROWN
Staff Writer

"I'm going to need a whole new wine list after this!"

With those words, Bob Thomas took a bottle of French wine and a bottle of Grey Goose vodka and ceremoniously poured the contents down the drain.

About 15 friends and supporters watched and applauded as the bottles emptied. Thomas tossed them into the trash bin and grabbed a bottle of Dom Perignon.

"What do you say we open 'er up?" he asked the group as he peeled back the seal. Thomas upended the bottle, purposely spilling the contents onto the bar where they flowed into a sink.

He then reached for another bottle and did the same.

While some might blanch at the thought of literally throwing away thousands of dollars in profit, what Thomas did Wednesday afternoon, March 19, at his Village Inn restaurant in Little Creek came as no surprise to his friends.

Frustrated by what he saw as the French government's attempts to protect its own interests in Iraq, Thomas said he decided to join other restaurant and liquor store owners throughout the United States in dumping his entire stock of French wines, champagnes and even mineral water in protest.

It was, he said, both a show of defiance against Paris and a gesture of support for the American troops that only hours later started their campaign to oust Iraqi dictator Saddam Hussein.

A lot of American youngsters will likely get hurt because of what France did to block attempts to get rid of Saddam and that, Thomas said, is what really aggravates him.

Living and working near Dover Air Force Base, the sight of C-5 Galaxy aircraft flying past is nothing new to the New York-born restaurateur and his wife, Cathy. The planes roaring overhead, many destined for Europe and the Middle East are a constant reminder to the couple of events transpiring thousands of miles away.

Thomas said he felt getting rid of his stock of French wines and liquors would be the best way he could both salute the servicemen and make a statement about the French government.

TO BAGHDAD

And to War

[Author's Note: Our battalion did a massive photo share when we returned from Baghdad. All of the photos in this section appear courtesy of the soldiers of Task Force $^1/_{15}$ Infantry.]

Email from Maggie dated March 22, 2003

Dear Friends and Family,

I just returned from a nine-day trip to Florida and did not have remote email access while gone. So many of you have called or emailed asking about JB that I thought I'd drop a note. Your prayers and concern have meant so much to Bob, Tyler, and me — we are grateful for your love and support. Some of you, also, have family over there. Please know that we are praying for you as well. (In fact, Nordy's son Jeffrey and his son-in-law were both deployed. Not sure exactly where they are except "over there.") JB is in the Third Infantry Division, First Battalion of the 15th Brigade. According to the Fox News website this morning:

"U.S. ground forces led by the Army's Third Infantry Division are likely to be at the outskirts of Baghdad by early next week."

So presumably, JB's on his way to Baghdad. The Third Division is known as the spearhead of the army. The 3rd ID's official website is http://www.stewart.army.mil/

My mom asked if we knew the colonel's name that JB is driving. We don't. I am hoping he is a "lead from the rear" kinda guy.

[Author's Note: No, he was not.]

Since JB drives a Bradley, please pray that JB gets time to sleep. When you are the only driver in the vehicle, you are always on duty. Sleep deprivation is a big issue.

[Author's Note: I did have an alternate driver. I just chose not to use him. It was my responsibility to get us there.]

Please continue to drop JB emails, letters, or cards. Who knows when he will get them, but I know they will be much appreciated.

Gratefully,
Maggie

Email from Maggie dated March 26, 2003

Dear All,
Yippee! A letter from JB! Although it was written before the war

began, it is soooo good to hear from him. Thank you all for your continued prayers and support! Please continue to write him — I've heard that some of the mail is making its way to the soldiers.

Blessings,
Maggie

Dear Mom,

I am reluctant to write this letter. Many reasons contribute to this reticence (which is a good word when you just used reluctant.) One of the primary reasons is my sincere doubt that this will even make it to you.

Let me give you a brief explanation of my current situation. [Editor's Note: Define *brief*.]

We have been kicked out of our kabal by the 101st Airborne Division, the screaming eagles, or as I refer to them, the "Grumpy Chickens." They have taken *our* places in our tents. The joke is that ol' LTC Charlton forgot to pay the rent and we were being evicted, but the laughter stopped on February 28 when the eviction notice was actually served, and we packed up for Operation Dragon Bedouin.

I cannot convey the bile in these words over paper without enclosing some actual bile. Or profanity, but I am adamant (great profanity substitute word!) about excluding such in my correspondence. The army can't beat me down on that one. But I need someone to talk to, metaphorically speaking.

We are in a nontactical assembly area, which is army for "a

spot in the middle of the desert." It is basically kabal jr. There is a berm, but it is little enough to jump over in a HMMWV (that's Humvee for those of you who went, huh?) and has no wire around it. It's enough of a joke that some units have actually used their ACEs (armored bulldozer) to cut their own "side doors" in the berm so they can take out the trash without having to go through the main gate and be bothered with whatever the password of the day is, usually something inane like "neck-brace rutabaga."

****

Hey army censors and pals! Those are not actual passwords so there is no need to bust out the black magic markers!!!

****

There are no showers. The chow is served from field chow trailers, which are frequently rendered inoperable by weather considerations or supply shortages. When we finally got tents up, we were packed in so thoroughly that the smell is only barely more tolerable than the elements.

The line companies don't even have tents for everybody, but even if they did it would hardly be relevant because of the Gigantic Mutant Killer Sandstorms of Agony!!!

I'm talking four feet of visibility. Inside the tent. Because we don't have floors in our tents, just good old "Desert Issue Item #1." Don't even bother going outside. If you don't have goggles your eyes will be relentlessly ground into pulp. If you do have goggles, all you will see is brown writhing natural hatred.

I woke up one morning unable to identify any of my personal property due to a uniform half-inch thick layer of brown dust on everything. And this was just from the dust contained inside the tent walls.

And I loathe to mention my smell. His name is Smell. Smell has its own personality and follows me around everywhere. Smell and I have a mutual respect for each other. I know if I take too huge a whiff of Smell, I'll actually become nauseous. Smell knows that if he irritates me too badly — e.g., being so strong as to actually prevent me from falling asleep — I'll flip out and kill him with soap and water bottles poured over my frigid naked body in the middle of the night.

We spar occasionally here and there. He'll make my eyes water and I'll retaliate with a strategic baby-wipe strike in the armpit and feet regions. Nevertheless, mostly I accept Smell's right to live and he stays contained within my double thick layer of uniform.

~JB

Letter from JB dated March 11, 2003

I have murdered Smell. He crossed the line last night when I was changing clothes to sleep. At first dark I placed a piece of wood next to my Bradley to keep sand off my feet and pounded a couple of pickets in front of it. Around these I wrapped a couple of ponchos, creating a makeshift shower curtain.

With the barrel of the 25mm traversed around to the nine o'clock position I was able to hang a makeshift shower bag and control the water flow by pinching a piece of plastic pipe inserted into the bottom of the bag.

It was perhaps the least pleasant shower I have every taken. Just in case the water wasn't cold enough for utter misery, the wind kicked up to make sure.

But when I was finished, Smell lay twitching on the ground, his last gasping words to me, "I thought we had an arrangement!" I felt no remorse and stepped off his carcass.

In case he tried to respawn [Editor's Note: I do not believe this to be an actual word] himself through the Smell-ettes that had been seeded through all my clothes, I dumped all my clothes in a bucket, poured water and detergent on them, and agitated. They came out stiff and pungent with soap, but they were (technically) clean. I expect this emotional high to last approximately three hours.

I am using these three hours to listen to the fabulous CD and read the equally fabulous letter I received yesterday evening from one Sarah Holmes. Thank you a thousand times over! This brings me to my closing concept.

Please continue to write, everyone. Although it is really no longer feasible to receive packages (I have gotten a few from some of you since I've been in this camp; they somehow slipped through the system), letters are arriving in a timely fashion. I am short on reading material as I had to pack up the bulk of my books into my storage box, which is currently in a huge container heading the *right* way across the Atlantic. [Editor's Note: JB without reading material is a sad and scary thought.] Letters and news from home are invaluable out here. I look forward to hearing from each of you.

~JB

P.S. [Editor's Note: This consists of a long paragraph asking me to send specific books and goggles.] I really miss all of you and have been thinking about you constantly since this deployment. Pizza and entertainment are on me when I get back!

P.P.S. Hey Mom, tell Sarah I'll buy her a plane ticket when I get back so she can come visit us when I am home on leave.

Dear Mom, Dad, and Miscellaneous Extras,
This letter should be rather more cheerful than the last. I am in a good mood, and I will tell you why. After reading that *Writer's Digest* magazine you sent me, I got to thinking about fiction competitions. (The issue you sent was their annual *Writer's Digest* fiction contest results for last year's competition.)

I read most of the winners in the short story categories, and I started thinking to myself, I can write as well as these people. I realized that it doesn't take some kind of expert in the field, like it does in, say, architecture or engineering, to write. It just takes somebody who is patient enough to write a whole bunch of stuff, edit it, rewrite it, and not get testy when somebody makes a correction or suggestion.

So exactly three days after reading the six winners in the genre and literary fiction categories, I printed out the final draft of my short story, "Death Comes to Nathan D. Alynnwood." (See appendix A for the text of this story.) Everyone I gave it to out here read it and visibly reacted to the ending, exactly as I'd hoped. I generated genuine human emotional response! How cool is that? A copy of the story is enclosed.

I got to thinking though, there's nothing that's stopping me from entering this in a competition, other than being stuck out here in the first circle of hell! Fortunately I have an infinitely patient and helpful mother, and I'm sure she'd handle the paltry details of sending out entry forms, etc., especially because I'm sending the addresses of the contests to her. (Please?)

Okay, this is where the letter gets somewhat stupid. Lots of stuff is happening out here, but it is all *secret*. So sorry, you'll have to wait until I return to get the delightfully exaggerated version of the story of the current U.S. presence in Kuwait.

Thank you very much for the goggles. They got to me immediately after I sent the letter wondering where my goggles were.

Sarah, the CD you sent is great. It was really nice to hear something different for a change. Your letter was awesome, and when I get home I'll probably frame it. It was good. I liked it.

Jeff Anderson: Sorry you are in Afghanistan. Bad luck, dude. I don't know who told you Bradleys have AC but they are imbibing controlled narcotics. That said, they will still take an RPG and keep rolling, so I'm glad to be on the inside of one.

Everybody else that I can't immediately think of something personal to say right now — don't die. I'll think of something when I come home and tell it to you, but you have to be alive. Okay?

Write me letters!!

~JB

[Author's Note: This portion of the book will differ slightly in format from the rest. The book is, of course, composed primarily of letters home. However, while we were attacking Iraq, I was so busy with other things — driving for hours on end each day, engaging the enemy, dodging and weaving through RPGs and indirect fire — that I really didn't have time to write any letters home.

I did, however, keep a journal. It was written exclusively in shorthand, and in looking back through it, now a year later, I don't always remember what I was talking about. But, dear reader, I have done my best to recreate the war through my eyes, and I've kept the same general format as my original journal, with a time-stamp on each entry. I have left many entries out because of their mundane nature. For example: drove for a million miles today; fantasized about inserting an MRE spoon into my gunner's eye; decided he might need that later to shoot some bad guys; refueled; pooped; went to sleep.

I also was in the habit of making a quick entry every time we had a meeting with the brigade commander, refueled, or met with the company commanders. This was useful for me later as far as keeping track of what visual memories go with what sections, but as there is not yet a printer on the market that can plug into my eye socket and print out my recollections, this doesn't really help you out very much. So I've left out all of those that didn't seem to pertain to the story. The photos included with my journal entries were all taken by soldiers in Task Force ¹/₁₅ Infantry.

So, without further ado, here is my best effort to show you the war through my eyes.]

🖇 🖇 JB's Journal, March 21, 2003

The first radio report received from the war went something like this:

Guy on radio: We're receiving reports of nearly 500 enemy troops closing in on our position. Everyone scan your sectors.

(Two minutes pass)

Guy on radio: Correction we're receiving reports of nearly 500 enemy camels closing in on our position. Gentlemen, this is *not* an opportunity for target practice.

Shortly afterwards, Marne 6 (our division commander) gave us some words of advice. I vaguely remember them being motivational. Essentially, it boiled down to don't stop shooting until five minutes after they stop shooting.

At approximately midnight, we received our final movement order. At 0317 Zulu/0617 local time, we crossed the berm into Iraq. This was the berm constructed after the Gulf War to establish the border between Kuwait and Iraq. Our engineers had been nice enough to leave us a little sign that said, "Welcome to Iraq" in case some of us had thought maybe we were headed to...Oman?

[Author's Note: We used Zulu time for a while. For those of you who don't know, Zulu time is short for Greenwich mean time, which is, of course, what time it is in Britain. The advantage to using Zulu time is that it can synchronize military operations across time zones. However, it is confusing because the time never lines up with what time it actually is, as far as eating, sleeping, etc. Also, Iraq is entirely in one time zone. For the first half of the war when you asked what time it was, you had to clarify whether it was "real" time or "pretend" time. Eventually we realized we were just being silly and we went to local time. From here on out, I'll just be using local time.]

The Iraqis didn't defend their border. This meant that essentially we got to hang out in enemy territory for a few hours by ourselves. This is the first leg of our incredibly long trek north. We took our first break to refuel and test fire our weapons. I've started my new hobby — littering. We can't exactly store our trash in the Bradleys. So I pop up my hatch occasionally and toss out MRE trash, water bottles, and baby wipes. And I don't feel guilty about it either.

Second Brigade made light contact. They engaged a couple of BMPs (Russian equivalent of a Bradley, only essentially without armor) and a T-55 (a great tank, if you lived in 1944). Three enemy vehicles versus a U.S. Army Brigade. We're taking tons of EPWs (enemy prisoners of war). Second Brigade's MPs are swamped. We're sending our MPs to assist.

We're told to expect our first enemy contact at Objective Firebird, which we expect to arrive at in 5 to 10 hours. The

Littering: One of the many joys of war.

colonel had a meeting to plan the attack. The line companies used this opportunity to air out their hapless dismounts. This would have been the first time the ramp had been dropped for them in nearly 12 hours. I took the opportunity to pop my hatch and dust off Hendershot (my little red puppy from Mellora).

We had already encountered several nomad tribes on our trip north. With their body language they tried to give us the impression they didn't care about us being here, but they all had white flags, even draped across their livestock.

1000: A dump truck surrendered to us. I'm not entirely sure why...

The terrain is getting more interesting. [Author's Note: I came to find out later that Iraq is not a barren wasteland, which is how I pictured a desert. This is, after all, the fertile crescent of the Bible, which is even more fertile now, thanks to massive irrigation.] At the risk of cursing myself, I commented to my gunner that the temperature, so far, has been bearable.

1243: Finished an MRE. An unexpected side effect of these long drives is that my butt keeps falling asleep. I'm surprised the army hasn't developed an "XM-38 Tactical Posterior Cushion for Combat Drivers." The radio report we received concerning a large number of displaced civilians turned out to be a large number of displaced goats. We gave them directions to Kuwait.

1430: We have our first encounter with Technical Vehicles, "Technicals." A Technical is an old, beat-up pickup with a bunch of guys with AK-47s and a machine gun on a mount made out of duct tape and PVC pipe in the bed. When your army won't buy you tanks... We destroyed them with artillery.

1450: Right now we are chilling out at our first attack position. I've decided to keep a log of my mileage. My starting odometer reading was 5,226k and I'm currently at 5,338k. [Author's Note: The long trek took its toll on my odometer, and it became increasingly inaccurate as time went by. No matter how fast I went, it advanced mileage as if I was going 5 kph. So I'm not going to bother including my mileage in this section.]

1517: We had our final meeting with the brigade commander before the attack on Objective Firebird. I used this opportunity to put some gas in my Bradley and take a nap.

1750: Our field artillery just unloaded about 25 missiles on some poor saps – I slept right through it. We've been stopped here in the assault position for a while. I am ready to move. War is boring.

2110: We've been driving for a while and have come to a three-lane highway. The colonel directed me onto the highway — but into the wrong lane. Of course medians aren't really an issue when driving a Bradley...so I ran over the guardrail into the correct lane. This is the most fun I've had so far.

2225: After a long drive down the highway we came to the outskirts of Al Nassirayah. This will be the site of our first firefight and some of the first real Iraqi Army resistance. It is strange to see a rather large city like this, with paved roads and tall buildings, and not a single car driving. Not that traffic would have been much of a problem for us. Tracked vehicles don't have to worry about who has the right of way.

2240: We've started receiving reports of skirmishes. It's mostly infantry, but we've had confirmation that there are a few BMPs moving around. From an objective standpoint, the tracer route flying through the air is visually very attractive — as long as they are traveling away from me.

2322: Our Bradley gets its first direct contact with the enemy. We fire our coaxial machine gun into a group that is trying to sneak up on us. This is before the Iraqis realize that we have night vision. We hit a few and the rest dropped their weapons and fled.

0010: Our tank company found an enemy motor yard (read: shooting gallery). You are technically supposed to destroy it with artillery, but they got bored waiting for the fire to be called in. It turns out a tank round can cut through four or five BMPs with one shot.

0017: Finished off the motor yard with a few artillery rounds. We're observing a BMP about 1,000 meters in front of us. The

March 21, 2003

2240: We've started receiving reports of skirmishes. It's mostly infantry, but we've had confirmation that there are a few BMPs moving around. From an objective standpoint, the tracer route flying through the air is visually very attractive — as long as they are traveling away from me.

2322: Our Bradley gets its first direct contact with the enemy. We fire our coaxial machine gun into a group that is trying to sneak up on us. This is before the Iraqis realize that we have night vision. We hit a few and the rest dropped their weapons and fled...

gunner really wanted to try firing a TOW missile but determined it had already been destroyed. I said, so shoot it anyway. He definitely won't miss.

After staring at the tank for a while we determined that it was cold and wasn't really any danger. We decided to put a couple of holes in it with our AP rounds so it couldn't be used against us. One through the turret and another through the engine block took care of that. Our sector was secure and I had a few hours to bed down before:

📎 JB's Journal, March 22, 2003

0639: Wakeup! After listening to the radio for a while I discovered that we had taken our first U.S. casualty. I wasn't sure, but it seemed like he was from our sister tank battalion. Never found out for sure if he was wounded or killed. Everybody seemed to be in quite a panic about this; I suppose they had figured we were going to go through the whole war without any casualties. This isn't training any more kids...

Objective Liberty, this "big picture" that our Objective Firebird was only a small part of, is still hot. Apparently some Iraqis have regrouped during the night and mounted a little counter offensive come daylight. We are standing by to assist if needed.

0808: We are called up to help — help gather EPWs. [Author's Note: This would, through the course of the war, prove to be one of the biggest hindrances to us. Every town we came through, whether we actually fought anyone or not we took huge numbers of EPWs. We had communications guys taking prisoners! I

felt badly for them; they looked as lost and confused as their prisoners.]

0920: I had my first experience with enemy mortar fire. We were securing some EPWs while we waited for the driver of our five-ton truck to come forward and take them off our hands. I was in front with my hatch open, reading a novel. Everyone else was out back, milling around trying to figure out exactly what to do with all these people. A mortar round exploded about 20 feet from my open ramp. I heard the noise, figured it wasn't there to help, and closed my hatch. Then I picked my book back up, figuring I'd finish the chapter by the time everyone figured out where to go and climbed back on the Bradley. The colonel took a boot to the face in the scramble to get in. Not sure it wasn't deliberate...

1000: Time for another gathering of the big shots. [Author's Note: I didn't really mind having to drive him all the way out to these impromptu command centers, because when we got there other people were responsible for the security and I could take a good two- to three-hour nap while all the brass chatted.]

This meeting was actually held in a captured Iraqi military headquarters. There were huge paintings of Saddam out front, one where he looked like Harrison Ford and another where he looked like General Patton. I wasn't sure if it was intentional or not.

Another long movement is planned for tomorrow, so I'm getting some sleep for the drive. I also stole a seat cushion from an empty seat in a Humvee to help keep my butt awake.

✎ ✎ ✎ JB's Journal, March 23, 2003

0504: Started our long movement by going in exactly the opposite direction for about a mile or so. I was a little upset with our fearless leader, but he blamed his GPS. The upside was we saw a really cool building. Some Iraqi architecture is pretty interesting — except for the uniform tan color scheme.

0641: One of our line companies stopped a white pickup; it was unarmed but somehow they had managed to acquire a U.S. Army tent. We confiscated it and we're still scratching our heads over how they managed to get one.

0727: Received reports that our sister infantry battalion had been ambushed by RPG teams wearing civilian clothing. [Author's Note: This was a big deal back then because we were, up until this point, only fighting uniformed soldiers.] About this time we received a change of mission — we had to

TO BAGHDAD

assist a cavalry unit that was taking excessive contact. We planned for another long movement.

1140: We paused briefly on our way to let one of our line companies clear a power station that was on the side of the road. We had a report that there may have been an RPG team hiding inside it. It was empty. I was becoming increasingly skeptical of "reports."

1200: Time to refuel! It amazes me to think about how much fuel we were using. My Bradley alone holds 300 gallons of fuel, and we refueled several times on any major movement, plus topped off regularly after running the colonel around on errands.

This refueling break turned into a long halt and a planning session.

1340: We moved about another 20 kilometers to meet with the commander of the cavalry unit. There was a huge open field with canals on three sides, which we turned into a motor pool. I suppose certain things are just ingrained in the military mind, because we really had no security to our formation. They literally set us up just like the motor pool back in Benning. It didn't seem like a good idea at the time.

1627: My good friend and counterpart Steven Santiago (he drove the major's Bradley) pulled up opposite me on the other side of a ditch. We amused ourselves by holding an impromptu puppet show using our hands and my stuffed dog Hendershot. I called the performance, "Five-Year-Olds at War," and unbeknownst to me, his gunner was taping me from the top of his turret.

1704: Our little motor pool formation obviously attracted some attention because we took several mortar rounds. It was horrible! The tanks and Bradleys were barely avoiding crashing into each other during the mad scramble to clear out of the area. I wound up raising my ramp, with the commander of the scout

section and the major, as well as the colonel in the back of my track. So, before we could hightail it out of there I had to play taxi and drop them off at their vehicles.

One vehicle was hit during the attack, and I was only amazed that it wasn't more. We were such a perfect target then. It's only by God's grace they didn't hit a group of vehicles. The vehicle that was hit was the medic track for our tank company. We escorted another medic track over to assist with the casualties. One medic was injured as well as the tank company's first sergeant, who was outside of the track when it was hit. He was thrown to the ground and immediately got back up. The first words out of his mouth were, "I'm okay, just gimme a bottle of water," before he passed out.

His body armor saved his life, although he did have shrapnel wounds on his arm and face. He was quickly evacuated to a hospital where he recovered safely.

I am definitely developing a sincere hatred for artillery fire at this point. We've found out that it's not like in the movies. It doesn't make the telltale whistling noise when it's coming at you. You can only hear it whistle if it is going by you. Basically, you only know when it's going to miss, not when it's about to hit you!

2035: It's been a long day. I'm exhausted, and I reek. Our chemical suits are amazing at keeping odors in. I found out just how much odor it was keeping in when I took off my jacket to change my sweaty t-shirt. The jacket went right back on.

2102: I couldn't hold it anymore. It was time to sneak out in the cover of darkness and take a dump. This was creepy; every little unfamiliar flash of light or noise caused me to start. Combat makes everything suck.

JB's Journal, March 24, 2003

0647: Woke up to the sound of mortars going off. I was immediately in high-alert mode (panic) and was starting to ready the vehicle to move out when our mortars came over the net to tell us that it was just them firing at the enemy. I have a real issue with their sequence. [Authors Note: This became a regular occurrence. Massive explosions, then a net call letting us know that it was no big deal, just some engineers blowing up an ammo cache, etc. Thanks for letting us know ahead of time...]

This morning I also found out that the first WIA we had received reports of was not a tanker as I had thought but a scout.

Apparently they had surprised an enemy force of about 75 personnel and gone ahead and engaged them. The scout Humvees are pretty heavily armed; each has either a 50 cal or an MK19, which is a belt-fed grenade launcher. The scout who was hit is in the hospital and doing alright. [Author's Note: Our medics were very efficient during the war, and they were never overloaded with casualties.]

1052: I saw our first major ammo cache destroyed. The engineers rigged the area with C4 and were even kind enough this time to give us a little heads up. The shockwave actually physically moved the Bradley, and my ears were ringing quite badly. It was incredibly awesome. We have to do this more often!

1500: We linked up with Able Company, who was scouting a route for the task force to take through this mazelike series of canals, railroad bridges, and fishing villages. We stopped and asked for directions from an old man in a hut all by himself. He actually spoke enough English to give us pretty good directions to a site where we thought we could make a crossing. The colonel gave him a battalion coin. I had to grudgingly admit that was a pretty classy thing to do.

On the way to the site we got into a firefight. Able began firing across the river, and we jumped right in also. Still not sure what we were shooting at, but we saw muzzle flashes and larger explosions across the way, which we thought could have been AT weapons. My soldier instinct was crying for me to take some kind of cover. I felt stupid sitting there looking at them through my periscopes. I fidgeted in my seat trying to get somewhere that felt like cover until my higher brain functions kicked in. Then I realized that I was in a Bradley, which was better cover than I could find by running outside and laying down behind a tree. I drive my cover with me wherever I go. I felt stupid for about half an hour after that.

1630: We had to abort the bridgecrossingapalooza. There's no way in the world we were going to get an entire task force across this bridge without incident. The tanks had maybe six inches of total clearance on either side when they tried to get across, and, as tired as everyone was, there was sure to be a mistake. As much as I loathed the extra hours of driving that taking the long way around entailed, I had to agree that it didn't justify losing a vehicle and the lives of its crew.

2100: A huge artillery barrage was unleashed. This was probably called in by brigade, or higher. I hope they were softening up our objective. This is also about the time people began discussing officially dropping the whole Zulu time thing. I wasn't the only one who realized it only added, never subtracted, confusion to the situation. Actually got to lie down for a good night's sleep.

📎 JB's Journal, March 25, 2003

0600: Good morning trooper! Pick up all this freaking trash around the Bradley! Apparently the colonel was pissed off about something else, so he relieved his anger by making us pick up the trash around the track, which we of course threw back on the ground when we got moving again. [Author's Note: As I mentioned earlier, there was *nothing else* we could do with it! Sometimes I wonder how many man-hours of labor the army has invested in tasks that it later has to undo.] Then I got depressed and listened to Cake's *Motorcade of Generosity*.

Today's mission is to attack an armor ambush that the Iraqis have apparently set up for this. How awesome is it to have intel so good that you know where the enemy's ambushes are and you can plan a coordinated attack on them?

[Author's Note: This was Mars Day as I like to call it. Most of you probably remember this from the news. Everything was suffused with this otherworldly orange glow. We were very surprised to see a dust storm here. The terrain wasn't the fine powdery sand we were used to from Kuwait. It was dirt and grass and mud, and I'm still trying to figure out how such an incredibly long-lasting and *thick* brownout kicked up so quickly and thoroughly. We found out later that the media was bemoaning the effects of the storm on troop movements, saying the effort was going to get bogged down. I'd like to know what unit they were with! We didn't slow down for a second. Granted, movements were more difficult with such limited visibility, but we kept on trucking to our objectives regardless.]

The Saddam Feydahyeen tried to take advantage of the storm to try to infiltrate past our front lines to our supply trains and cause mayhem. They were unsuccessful, thanks to high vigilance by our line units and probably because our supply chains — though lightly armed by our standards — have more firepower than most Iraqi Regular Army units!

1609: We were briefly paused at an intersection while we reorganized and brought the supply lines forward so we could better protect them. Out of the orange curtain a pickup truck comes barreling down the road. It was filled front and back with Feydahyeen dressed in their all black "ninja suits" and bristling with AKs! More trucks followed close on their tail. We tried to fire,

but even with the barrel as low as mechanically possible, we were so close that we were aiming over their top!

Fortunately, coming up behind us was our tank company. We radio them about the oncoming trucks, and waited. Several tank rounds and lots of 50 cal blasting later, they called us back. The conversation went something like this:

Tank Commander: That's it. We got all four of them.

Colonel: Excellent. I want you to search the vehicles now for anything important.

Tank: Search what? There are no vehicles.

Colonel: The four vehicles you just engaged!

Tank: Sir, those were 120mm tank rounds we fired at a pick-up truck. All I see is a hole in the ground and what looks like the steering wheel. That might be a hubcap about 50 yards away.

Want me to bring you the steering wheel? You can search it yourself.

Lesson learned: even ninjas can't survive a 120mm high-explosive round.

1611: We received a report of a friendly fire incident. [Author's Note: It later turned out to be false. I was amazed that in all this poor visibility all we had was a single close call, and no one injured or killed from friendly fire in our unit. Once again God shields us from the enemy...and ourselves.]

2042: The night of mud is finally over. I am tired, drained, and exhausted. We just finished breaking track on the vehicle. The colonel directed me down a dead-end alleyway, and instead of backing us up he wanted me to make an incredibly sharp turn around and go. Now, the Bradley is capable of this — on pavement. But when you're on mud, it piles up in the track and suspension and can actually force the track off its guides. This is what happened to us. Everyone was highly upset with everyone else, but now it's done and I can rest. I can only hope this dust is gone when I wake up...

1038: Spent the day in a tactical assembly area. Visibility is still bad, although not as bad as before. We are considering loading the tracked vehicles onto heavy equipment trucks (HETs) for our next movement. This will save a lot of wear and tear on the tracks and the vehicle in general. I can only assume this is because our route is already secure?!

The colonel came back in an eerily good mood. He explained that this may be our last big stop before we mount an assault on Baghdad. He wanted to be part of the force assigned to take Baghdad more than anything else. Looks like he's getting his wish. I'm up for the trip too. Doesn't capturing the capitol mean you win the war? Right? Right? *Right?*

1440: Years of video games have honed my fast-twitch muscle response to the level that was required for today's drive. Thirty feet of visibility, an extremely high rate of speed, two-way traffic, and sudden drop-offs in the road combined to make me a nervous wreck by the time we stopped. The gunner actually congratulated me upon completion of the drive. "Good job putting up with him," he said. For once it wasn't just him stressing me out, though.

We took some Iraqi Special Forces prisoners and found maps, radios, phone numbers, etc. in their hideout. Hopefully this intel will save U.S. lives.

We are linking up with the Second Brigade now. Our brigade has detached us to assist them because they are now taking point. It was our good fortune to be the spearhead for Third Infantry Division the entire war.

1543: We had a false alarm chemical attack. That was a frightening time. Chem was a big scare for us, despite all our fantastic armor, weapons, and vehicles. We knew that we were likely to die if we were gassed, despite our protective masks and chemical suits. Everyone knew it, but no one really wanted to say it.

1600-2100: We've had sporadic contact all day. Mostly skirmishes; we're still getting ready to move to the big fight.

2121: I've finished another excruciating seat-of-my-pants

drive. We had several near collisions. We're stopping for the night. Tomorrow's destination will be "the escarpment."

0500: Moving out...

0748: Had an exciting event during the movement. We had to travel through a series of winding roads with irrigation ditches on either side. On the far side of one of the ditches an Iraqi covered truck was parked. It had obviously been hit and disabled so we didn't pay much attention to it — until it emitted a loud *fwoosh* and a vapor trail streaked out from it.

The truck contained rockets and they just happened to heat to the cook-off point as our convoy passed. I don't think I've ever braked with such a sense of purpose and resolution before. The truck was loaded, and the rockets kept coming. However, waiting until the last one finished before moving was not an option either; this was a hot zone, and the entire convoy would become a giant target for a sneaky individual with some motivation and an RPG, so we had to leapfrog past the truck.

It was like something out of an old side-scrolling video game. We crept up as close as we felt was safe, waited until a rocket cooked off, then hightailed it across the danger zone, another rocket screaming across the road where we had been just seconds ago. Phew! God certainly protected us and our entire convoy, as there was no real rhyme or reason to how the rockets cooked off. Sure, we felt better thinking that we were timing it just right and doing it ourselves, but there's no real reason two rockets couldn't have gone off one right after the other.

0848: I get my first look at the escarpment. This is a massive hill blocking our way. There is only one single lane road leading over and through it, and it is flanked on either side by canals. The escarpment forced everyone into a single file line. [Author's Note: At the time, I thought it'd be an excellent defensive point for the Iraqis since it was such a great choke point. Now I realize that we could have easily taken out any defensive position with close air support (CAS) because they would have been highly exposed on the flat top of the hill. We passed through agonizingly slowly but without incident.]

0950: We passed a unit that had just suffered a head-on collision between a fueler truck and a soft-top Humvee. It was not a pretty sight.

1000: We met up with some cool Special Forces guys. We talked to them for a while, trading stories. Much to my gunner's delight, he was even able to score a can of dip. [Author's Note: He was a lot easier to deal with while that lasted.]

1027: Next target on our list — Karbala. This is the last stop between us and Baghdad. We've received reports that the Republican Guard has ambushes set up for us. There is also apparently some major bridge that they are going to detonate if we start crossing it. Still, the mission goes on. The army certainly can't cancel because the enemy is supposed to be in the area...

The rest of the day is spent preparing troops, weapons, and vehicles for the battle. Many plans are proposed, discussed, and finally set in place.

1128: We continue to plan and prepare. We're having some serious issues with the turret. The master gunner comes and completely takes apart our 25mm chain gun's feeding mechanism, down to the tiny springs. Hopefully it'll be working now.

We received a report that an unmanned aerial vehicle found an enemy track and a couple of rocket launchers. They were destroyed by CAS.

1309: Tomorrow we'll be moving to Karbala. I took an opportunity to use the colonel's satellite phone to call home. My mom was thrilled to hear that I was safe and well. The phone is mounted in the back of his Humvee, driven by my close friend SPC (at the time) Potocki.

Potocki was my wheeled-vehicle counterpart. He drove the Colonel around in his Humvee. Potocki was a really deep thinker and also something of a neatnik. This led to some conflict with the Colonel, who every morning would check his reflection in the side mirror of the Humvee. Instead of moving his face to the mirror, he'd move the mirror to his face, of course moving it hopelessly out of alignment and rendering it useless for the driver. But that's another story...

[Author's Note: Potocki and I didn't see much of each other

during the war because the wheeled vehicles weren't usually with the tracks, but on occasion we'd have a couple hours to hang out and attempt to use this phone. It was an incredibly long process that involved entering nearly a hundred numbers to configure the cryptographics of the system, then trying to navigate through the phone system to connect to the DNS military phones in Kuwait, which could connect me to a DNS phone at Dover Air Force Base near my house, where I could speak to an operator who could dial me out to a civilian line. It took ages to get through and actually have a stable enough connection that you could have a 10-minute conversation back home. But I have no complaints; the vast majority of the soldiers had no access to a phone whatsoever, so I was grateful for a few minutes to alleviate my mom's worries.]

I went to bed shortly after my gunner told me, "Get some sleep. Lots of people will be shooting at each other tomorrow."

"Looking good!"

0600: Time to go to Karbala. We maneuvered through a series of farms and canals and also some major roads. The tracks had no problem passing over the irrigation pipes, but there were old tank ditches and giant holes hidden in the fields, presumably left over from the Gulf War, because they didn't look fresh. One Able Company track managed to fall halfway into one. Damage assessment: PVT Rodriguez was furious that his CD player was destroyed in the crash.

0835: My gunner spots an RPG team sneaking around by a farmhouse. We are about 300 meters behind the front lines, moving to link up with the Able Company commander. We stopped to engage the team, and he manages to hit one of the enemy troops with an AP round. Our HE, which is what you would want to use against a small target like that, was not working. It was an incredible shot, and I was duly impressed. He described the results of the AP round connecting with the RPG trooper like stomping on a tomato.

[Author's Note: I made no entries after this until the morning of April 2, 2003. The trek up to Karbala was a tedious two-day process with many minor skirmishes along the way. I know this should be the exciting part, but really it was mostly tedious. We had to advance cautiously and thoroughly clear every suspect enemy fighting position. Every firefight was about three seconds of spine-tingling excitement followed by tedious searching and maneuvering, like a giant chess game. Finally we were in the outskirts of Karbala. Karbala itself was also an extended battle. My journal entries were kind of sporadic and the chronology was also a little confusing. This is a condensation of my entries for Karbala, and it's written retrospectively.]

JB's Journal, 0900 March 30, 2003 through 1033 April 2, 2003

The Battle of Karbala was a good practice for Baghdad. We spent more time moving vehicles in and through urban streets than we had in An Nassirayah and Al Samawah. The terrain was actually kind of nice, in an absolute perspective, although tactically it was a real bear.

There was a canal network throughout the entire city. Not

canals like you might find in Venice as a method of transportation. The canals were smaller and they paralleled nearly every road. There were also some larger canals that formed the backbone of the system, which required medium-sized bridges to cross. This slowed our movements and caused bottlenecks.

But the canals make for much more fertile ground that sustains a lot of bushes and other vegetation, including palm trees. It looked like it could be a nice place to live, with its attractive greenery and stone footpaths to allow pedestrian traffic across the gridlike canal network. The houses appeared sturdier and better constructed than many of the residential and farming areas we had seen before. We also noticed a huge increase in car ownership. The population was obviously wealthier (relatively speaking) here than in southern Iraq.

The first day we made some recon-by-fire movements into the city. The ¹/₁₅ INF spearheaded this movement. We quickly discovered that the terrain prevented the units behind us from supporting us in any way. We sent our three line units in, on line down parallel streets and did our best to flush out any enemy resistance.

We had numerous firefights and they all kind of blur together in my mind. One asset that we were fortunate to have was a psi-ops (psychological operations) and civilian affairs team. The psi-ops Humvee had a massive speaker system mounted to the top and blared a repeating message in Arabic telling the citizens to stay indoors so they were not mistaken for enemy troops. It worked pretty well. Indoors to them also seemed to include their yard, but they were cautious about appearing nonthreatening and just seemed to want to see what was going on. It made it much easier for us to determine who had hostile intent, especially because none of the average citizens drove their cars anywhere.

When we had cleared over halfway into the city, we did a kind of three-pronged U-turn and headed back to our assembly area outside Karbala. It was determined that it would be foolish to try to set up any kind of camp inside the city. Since we are not a light unit, we have the luxury to put some distance between us and our objective when we are resting up for another day of fighting.

Because of the distance between us and the city it meant only the most dedicated resistance fighters were willing to make the trek out to attack our perimeter at night. With our thermal capabilities we saw them long before they were a threat and were able to defeat all of them before they made it within small-arms range.

Bright and early the next morning we were rolling down the streets of Karbala. This time, Second Brigade's tank battalion was given the lead to allow us a little break. We heard the reports of their main guns and the .50 cal throughout the day, and I could tell it was killing the colonel that he couldn't join the fight. Personal feeling aside, I had to give the guy credit; he was dedicated to winning the war, and he was dedicated to keeping his Task Force alive. We didn't suffer a single fatal casualty.

Tusker, a tank battalion from Ft. Stewart, got into some pretty heavy firefights and found numerous ammo caches as they worked their way to the north end of the city. To take the burden off them and allow their units to stay in the fight, we took over security on these sites until the engineers could move forward to us and start blowing them. That got the civilians to stay in their homes even better than the psi-ops Humvee had. They didn't like having their teeth rattled out of their head apparently.

The Battle for Karbala ended that final day and we stayed in the Karbala Gap. This was it, tomorrow was Baghdad or bust!

This was the day of the notorious, at least to us, Objective Saints. I wish I could sit down four random soldiers from each of our companies and have them type just one story into my computer. Both vehicle crews and dismounted infantry fought long and hard all day today. There were more examples of heroism and bravery today than will ever be fully known. I hope that these soldiers, some of them Silver- and Bronze-Star awardees, get the chance to make their story known someday.

For me, however, Saints was an embarrassment and a shame. That morning the turret barfed up a large electric spark and the whole system died on us. No commo, no big gun, no GPS — nada! The colonel had to jump to another track from one of the line companies.

We followed but we were essentially a giant small-arms platform. Our firepower dropped from a 25mm chain gun and a 7.62mm machine gun to an M16 and a firing port weapon, which isn't even designed to be fired by hand!

But we fought on. We even managed to flush an RPG team out of their cover and into the firing sector of a M113 that had a 50 cal on it, which destroyed them.

But the shame came that night when the crew of the vehicle that the colonel had commandeered was chilling out and swapping stories with us. The colonel, in his usual way, had brought them to every major firefight in the battalion, and the gunner had seen tons of action. I felt sorry for my gunner for once; I could see his face getting red as the stories were told. That action should have been his responsibility.

That day, the TOC, which is where all my friends from headquarters who I didn't see much of during the war worked, took mortar rounds. I was so relieved when I finally found no one was hurt.

We camped in a grassy depression on the side of a major highway. The mechanics got to work fixing our electrical system.

The mechanics don't have all the parts they need to finish repairs. I now have to jumpstart my vehicle whenever we need to run from one area to another. Please fix my Bradley!

We move underneath the cloverleaf highway intersection. This is about 200 meters from our previous position. We ran into some more Special Forces, and once again they resupplied my poor gunner with dip. I had to be happy for him — he looked like a kid on Christmas day!

I also saw good old Steven Santiago, my counterpart, today. But it wasn't all fun and games. This was where one of our soldiers lost his foot to a DPICM, a dual-purpose improved conventional munition. They are one of our munitions fired from the Paladin field artillery pieces. They are about the size of a D battery, and this one hadn't detonated on impact. Unfortunately, the warhead was still functional and one of our soldiers — either a scout or a mortar I can't remember — found it. He was evacuated to Germany.

✐ ✐ ✐ JB's Journal, April 7, 2003

Today we decided that we had been in the same place for too long and moved to an old industrial compound. I'm not sure we ever determined its former function, but it appeared to be a gravel or asphalt plant of some kind. It also — bonus — had a huge missile hidden in a cargo contained nearby! What a great place to stay! Especially comforting was the fact that it did not appear to be assembled by actual rocket scientists. Some of the rivets were only partway in or missing altogether, and, maybe it was just me, the fins did not appear to be spaced evenly around the body. Please don't let this thing get hit by a mortar...

Speaking of missiles, one hit our old position shortly after I left. Later, when we drove by on our way to a mission, I noticed that the crater was practically centered on the place where I had my Bradley parked a day earlier. Insert spinal tingling here...

Sadly this was the missile attack that killed a few troops and that reporter; I don't remember his name. I wasn't exactly watching the news at night at the time, but I remember hearing about it later. Our tank company was also attacked by some smaller rockets, but fortunately they were about 300m off target.

We experienced extended contact with the enemy throughout the day, but we heard that the supply chains had pushed up the parts we needed for my Bradley. The mechanics repaired it — back in the saddle at last!

JB's Journal, April 8, 2003

Today we entered the matrix — our objectives are called Trinity, Neo, and The Oracle. Seriously, how cool is that? Trinity and Neo are huge cloverleaf overpasses, one of which also has a huge shopping complex to secure, and Oracle is an open area with a lake and a racetrack of some kind. The Iraqis were obviously surprised to see us this far this quickly. We captured one high-ranking enemy officer — think Pentagon equivalent — who was driving down the highway on his way to work!

Our mission was to recon these objectives and several smaller ones, but our troops were moving so aggressively that we kept taking and securing instead of just observing them. Our colonel was thrilled, and the dedicated and fearless action of our task force helped speed up the timetable of the Battle of Baghdad by several days!

Castle discusses federal budget, post-war Iraq

By JEFF BROWN
Staff Writer

Battles of two kinds — budgetary and military — were on Rep. Mike Castle's agenda Friday April 4, during a noontime visit to his Dover office. The state's lone congressman discussed efforts to approve the FY 2004 budget appropriations bill as well as the ongoing war in Iraq, where, he noted, Delaware had just suffered its first casualties.

One of only 12 Republicans to vote against the budget bill, Castle said he objected to the measure because it called for reductions in Medicare, Medicaid and veterans' programs, among others. As the country is facing difficult economic times, Congress should rightfully decline to increase spending, Castle said, but should also avoid cutting into necessary programs.

The measure eventually passed in the House by a three-vote margin, and was sent to a committee to iron out differences between it and a Senate version. Castle said he hopes the committee is able to finalize the package before Congress adjourns for its Easter recess April 11.

Castle is also hoping for a quick resolution of differences over President George Bush's proposed tax cut. The measure is stalled in Congress over differences in the House's $726 billion version and the Senate's $350 billion package.

The United States expects to have other nations share in what Castle indicated would be "significant costs" in the rebuilding of Iraq. Some of those costs are contained in a recently approved $77.9 billion wartime supplemental appropriations bill.

"This is not just money that is being handed over to somebody, it is money which is in large part being spent, in some way or another, in America," he said. "If the war ends, if we actually get a small but effective stimulus package, if we go through rebuilding to a degree, my view is all of this will be helpful with respect to our economy."

The nation has some serious economic problems, many of which have been ignored for the time being due to the war on terrorism, Castle said. These are problems, he said, that Americans must face in the very near future.

LIBERATION

Dictatorships are so 1940

✐ ✐ ✐ JB's Journal, April 9, 2003

Trinity, Neo, and the Oracle are in u.s. hands now, and we are seeing the light at the end of the tunnel. We set up camp in a man-
made lake near a massive mosque. I decided to bathe in the lake,
and would have even taken a little swim if Steven hadn't stopped
by and said, "Snakes..." and tapped his nose knowingly. I was out
of the lake mere seconds later. We spent the evening sharing stories and a cigar while sitting on the engine hatch of his Bradley. The
mosque played a haunting dirge/wail over its speakers while the
artillery shells fell on the city in the background. It was surreal.

By the end of the evening many major government buildings were occupied by u.s. forces and anti-Saddam Iraqis. The
Iraqis were rejoicing in the streets, bringing the troops sodas and

FROM BASIC TO BAGHDAD

cigarettes, and little girls came up to ask for autographs and to give us flowers.

Today we start a food giveaway program. Very little enemy activity at this point. We are mostly doing civil affairs missions. Today we raided two military buildings. The first was a customs station, and we found hundreds of weapons and countless rounds of ammunition. We loaded it all into an abandoned dump truck and blew it up. I also found time to piss on a painting of Saddam and grab a few Iraqi books and keys as souvenirs.

The second building was an Iraqi uniform warehouse. This means... SOCKS FOR EVERYONE! Praise God for that. It is impossible for me to describe how bad our feet were and how rancid our socks were becoming. I walked out of there with armfuls of brand new comfortable socks and gave some to Potocki and Steven.

✎ JB's Journal, April 12, 2003

Today we found a terrorist/spy training camp. We found records of their special women's training program, and the candidates looked like Americans or Europeans — blonde, fair skinned, not Arab in appearance at all. I wonder if these agents have managed to infiltrate our government.

There were also about a billion trillion weapons here. We've run out of explosives, so we're stuck guarding them until we can come up with a better solution. There are too many here to run them all over with our tanks.

Today we also got into a firefight in an intersection by a commercial sector. We found that we were fighting Jordanian and Syrian mercenaries, according to their ID cards. A suicide bomber tried to kill the master gunner and the colonel's ratelo. Fortunately, they had him facing against a brick wall for searching when he pulled open his bomb vest. They were both knocked on the ground, and the master gunner can't hear too well at this point, but they were both fine otherwise. [Author's Note: To this day, the master gunner still has difficulty hearing.] We were all shaken up for a while afterwards.

Some of the mercenaries play dead, lying in the street waiting for soldiers to pass by and then opening up on them. Fortunately, their marksmanship is terrible, but we've had several close calls. They fight dirty. We're lucky they haven't managed to take any civilians as human hostages; that's a terrible situation.

We're back to civil affairs type missions. The citizens are trying to resume their lives, traffic everywhere. Getting around is like a real-life game of *Crazy Taxi*. I'm terrified I'm going to run

someone over because I can't see them. They don't seem to understand I need more space around me than one of their little cars. I can only do my best...

These people really aren't so bad, and they're thrilled to have been freed from that madman. They can finally start schooling again because we've cleared all the weapons out of the grade schools where he was storing them. We also burned the textbooks because they showed cartoons of people beating Kurds to death and other such propaganda.

Maybe soon the kids can go back to school.

We've taken up residence in a Ba'ath party home by a canal. This is where we'll be for the rest of our time in Baghdad. Our uniform has downgraded drastically, no more body armor. We walk around in our brown t-shirts and, on occasion, sandals. My duties now consist mostly of radio duty as the colonel can now safely take the Humvee to meetings and civil affairs sites.

[Author's Note: This was my last entry. I was able to begin writing on a computer again, and I even printed out a few letters to send home while we were in the canal house.]

Email from Maggie dated May 1, 2003

Hi All,

Just a quick JB update. He called twice last weekend — missing us both times.

The first time he said he was coming home May 15. The second call said never mind. Orders were changed, and they now have stabilization and police-keeping duties for at least a few more months. He said mail was getting there now, and he really, really, really appreciates letters! Small packages are great too. And, of course, prayers are still requested on his behalf.

Thanks!

Maggie

Hi All!

Praise the Lord — JB just called and is fine! He is in the Baghdad suburbs doing peacekeeping duty. Right now that means he is mostly on the radio. He is living in a liberated house — one that was liberated from Ba'ath party officials. JB thinks he will be able to call much more frequently now that they have phones set up — the connection was great!

He was so thankful for all the letters and packages he's been receiving. The letters mean so much to the guys there. He said he's gotten great packages from the Smiths, Silers, DePaces, and some folks he doesn't know, including a young lady in Illinois (I think) and a group of students his Uncle Bill works with in Florida. And more, but he couldn't remember them all off the top of his head. He asked me to pass on his thanks.

They will be there probably a few more months. It is getting very hot. His sleeping space is on the roof of the house and he bakes there. He'd love more mail! If you do send packages, keep them small, like the size of a small shoebox. (Trail mix, granola, cereal bars, and beef jerky are wonderful, and he'd love some new music CDs.)

He's had quite a few experiences, although most of them are not funny. Toppling a 25-foot bronze statue of Saddam in his Bradley was a highlight though! Yes, he's been in quite a few palaces. He said the stuff in them is great by Iraqi standards but kind of cheap by ours. The chandeliers he saw were made of plastic.

He was actually assigned to the Second Brigade for a while and managed to be a part of two of the major spearheads: one by the First Brigade and one by the Second. Lots of RPG and artillery fire nearby, but God certainly protected him many times over.

Right now things are getting tense there with civilians wanting the u.s. presence gone. This is why they aren't coming home right away, although they have been packed up to go for a while now.

JB says to tell his friends (they know who they are!) that he has gotten more mail from strangers than from his best buddies at home. I told him they were probably busy with finals. He said "Yeah, and I'm busy with a war…"

He is going to try and call as much as he can this week now that he has access to a phone.

Bob and I so appreciate your prayer support for him!

~Maggie

Letter from JB dated May, 2003

[Editor's Note: JB wrote this letter in May, but he didn't mail it until June 27.]

Dear Home,

Once again I am reduced to scribing another desert epistle. I was really hoping not to have to write another one because it so thoroughly reminds me that it will be a while before I get home.

Two days ago we were expecting the advance party to leave

in the morning and us to follow in two days. But the next morning I awoke to see the advance party vehicles still in their parking spaces and their drivers unconscious in their cots. So I was upset. Right now we are looking at another couple of weeks so I've decided to pass some time with a letter. Hopefully I'll make it home before this does.

We are basically mission complete here in Iraq. We have been relieved by 1st AD (Armored Division) on all of our control points and are waiting for HETs (big honkin' trucks). They tend to get lost. Okay, granted, it is like a twelve-hour drive, but honestly, there is only ONE TURN to make and after that you just follow the stupid highway all the way until you reach the big "Welcome to Baghdad" sign, and then you make a left. Hey truck drivers — we'll be the ones standing there cheering for you!

Thirty HETs managed to make the trek last night and the different companies were literally fighting each other to get their vehicles loaded on. It turns out that the HETs were there for disabled vehicles (i.e., vehicles with huge gaping RPG and Howitzer holes in their engine blocks), and all the functional vehicles had to be taken back off the HETs and the broken ones lifted into place. By lifted I assume they just grabbed 50 privates and told them to heave-ho. Aspirin for everybody...

Now they are telling us that, once again the advance party is leaving in the morning. We should not be too far behind, but I am no longer in a speculative mood. We'll get back when we get on that plane.

This time the dreaded "Lot 5" should be of reduced intensity. We only get two days at the wash rack, and we won't be doing any actual maintenance on the vehicles. We'll just turn in a list of parts and deficiencies and then scram. I hope, anyway. My vehicle is thoroughly monkey feces right now, and I seriously doubt it could drive farther than the Karbala Gap from here. My Bradley would be excruciating to fix, nearly everything needs to be replaced or tweaked. Ideally, I could turn in a deficiency form that reads...

Need:

One Bradley Fighting Vehicle (complete)

But I don't want to think about it either way. If turn-in is a gimme, great. If not, there's always psychosis. You can never say you don't have options.

And on a lighter note, your letters and packages are truly phenomenal! I've been trying to hold on to as many addresses as possible so I can write to you when I get out of this desert and back into a real country with consistent plumbing, electricity, and an economy. To the girl who sent me the Twizzlers: you are cool, and even though I was raised not to talk to or accept candy from strangers, I make an exception for you! [Editor's Note: Oh sure, he remembers this part! What about the part about not playing with guns?]

To Reed DePace: okay, the repeating package thing is getting creepy. I'm starting to suffer really awful déjà vu. Oh, and Larry Niven is great. I'd never read him before, but since the *Integral Trees*, I've been stealing him from the MWR libraries. [Editor's Note: Surely this is a figure of speech. I know he was taught the Thou Shalt Not Steal part too...] [Author's Rebuttal: Since I'm the only soldier in my unit who can read, I always assumed they were there for me.]

Mom, I don't know how you knew that G.K. Chesterton would precisely hit the spot. I had forgotten how much I enjoy his work and the *Flying Inn* is probably the funniest I've read yet. [Editor's Note: Mom is beaming.] It has reminded me that

"Thursday" needs to become a screenplay; I wish I had my copy of it out here so I could start. Tell Mr. Stout to read it. I guarantee he'll see the same potential in it.

I've gotten other awesome packages from the Silers, Rakes, Woods, Lanes, and lots more. I can't thank you guys enough!

And that's it. I can't wait to get home for leave. Right now, the tentative leave dates are June 1 to June 14, but additional leave will be authorized for those who have the days and I should have plenty of days. I plan to take three weeks. I'll miss the fourth of July, but I don't want to use up too much of my leave.

So, until next time,

JB

Post-Scriptorium:
I just finished a grueling 30-hour nerd-fest working on converting all our map graphics for the whole war onto new map software. It is the Quark of the army. [Editor's Note: Quark is the page layout software used by many publishers.]

It was so ludicrously complicated that I spent one hour learning the basic drawing tools and then applied my knowledge for 15 minutes before I could make a single line appear — and then it was pointing the wrong way.

However, the three of us kept at it until we had a basic familiarity with the program and we were able to eventually finish the entire map. The next day we were publicly thanked and received battalion coins. It was nice to get a little recognition.

The maps were for our Presidential Unit Citation package, which is the highest unit-level award. We were happy that we were critical to the unit actually receiving this award before the year is out.

June 24, 2003

Hey Mom and Dad...and Everyone,
Back in Kuwait for the third time...

Phone access is sporadic at best so don't expect a call for a while. We have finally received, brace yourselves, permission to leave. I didn't realize that was even an issue. But dates are still in the far future. We're seeing things like August... September... whenever the other brigades get back... never...

So it really stinks over here. I received a bit of mail recently. Sarah H. sent a letter. It was the "red" themed one. I got one from Rick Barr that had fantastic pictures in it. I was in tears when I saw myself in all my long-haired, bass-wielding glory. How far I have fallen...

Hi All,

This email is just in from JB — that's right — an email! Now you have a *really* easy way to write him and it sounds like he could use the encouragement...

His address is faintpremonition@yahoo.com.

Blessings,

Maggie

Hey Mom and Dad...and Everyone,

Back in Kuwait for the third time...

Phone access is sporadic at best so don't expect a call for a while. We have finally received, brace yourselves, permission to leave. I didn't realize that was even an issue. But dates are still in the far future. We're seeing things like August... September... whenever the other brigades get back... never...

So it really stinks over here. I received a bit of mail recently. Sarah H. sent a letter. It was the "red" themed one. I got one from Rick Barr that had fantastic pictures in it. I was in tears when I saw myself in all my long-haired, bass-wielding glory. How far I have fallen...

Luke sent a really interesting one too. It was like having a conversation with him right here, or at least listening to him babble.

He was right about one thing though, he perfectly described how I would read the letter — "as lazily as possible."

If you didn't understand any of the previous paragraphs, *it's probably because you're not the intended audience*!

And moving right along, in Kuwait they have weird flavors for their snacks. I ate a popsicle that was "rose" flavored and had "chips" made from corn and potato that claimed to be "prawn cocktail" flavored. I ate exactly two of them.

Nothing else is happening. If we are going to be out here much longer, I may purchase an X-Box to help pass the time. If only there was a way to plug it directly into my eye sockets instead of having to scrounge a TV.

If you have time to email, please do so. I check mine about every two or three days, and I'm able to average about two responses back before I run out of time. I'll see you guys... later.

All hail the conquering hero...

~JB

Email from JB dated July 10, 2003

Hey,
The flight date looms closer and closer. I probably won't email again until I get back to the States. A couple things that you could do for me:

How much money do I have exactly in my account? Email me today if you get a chance.

Does the church have a projector that connects to a computer?

If so, it'd be really cool if I could borrow it. It'd be the easiest way to show all these war photos. They are all digital.

Stock the fridge in about two and a half weeks. I *need*: Sub stuff. Lots of roast beef, salami, provolone, and vinegar. Blue cheese dressing, feta cheese, and that bread in the purple package. Pizzas. Big ones with lots of stuff on them. Or ingredients to make my own. Steak and other cow products to grill, fry, or sautee. Mushrooms, onions, and enormous quantities of macaroni and cheese. Ice cream, involving peanut butter and various chocolates whenever possible. Chicken pot pie. And unhealthy cereals of all kinds. And bagels with various flavors of cream cheese. That's all I can think of for now, but I'm sure I'll send an addendum.

See you all soon.

~JB

Email from JB dated July 11, 2003

Hey,

More food I've been thinking about:

- Yogurt — the fruit on the bottom kind, in large quantities of various flavors
- Granola bars — crunchy in assorted flavors
- Frozen fruit — to make shakes
- Lasagna

We are finally getting out of this kabal tomorrow. So this is the really really real last email from out here. The planes should get here pretty soon. I can't wait to get home. Right after we land we will get our rooms and then receive 48 hours off. Unfortunately, this is before we get household goods or anything. I will probably stay in Benning rather than trying to visit anybody. Leave will be about 10 days after the 48 hours after whenever we land. It's like trying to predict the Apocalypse, lots of clues — no start point...

So anyway. There's not much else to say. You can still email me today; I may get on one last time before we get out of here tomorrow. Otherwise I'll call you from Georgia.

~JB

Email from Maggie dated July 13, 2003

Hi All,

Praise the Lord! JB is on u.s. soil! He just called from an airplane at JFK! (He's sitting in first class. Soldiers who volunteered to load luggage on board got to sit there.)

His leave will be sometime around the very end of July or the first few weeks of August.

Yippee! And thanks soooooooo much for all your prayers. Let's keep the rest of the guys still there in prayer.

~Maggie Hogan

First-timer enjoys State Fair on the cheap

By ESTHER WHIELDON
Staff Writer

Hot wisps of hay-and-cotton-candy-scented air float over vehicles in the Delaware State Fair parking lot.

Before one clears the entrance gate he or she can hear game vendors taunting, see a rainbow of rides flinging people in the air, and smell the excitement of a day full of food, agriculture and entertainment.

Any first time visitor to the Delaware State Fair, such as myself, who recently moved to Dover from Washington, D.C., will quickly learn that the sensory overload of promises are easily kept once inside the gate.

A free shuttle will get one quickly acquainted with most of the fairgrounds. That is if you manage to flag one down. Don't be afraid to whistle or holler if the shuttle zips by without stopping. On a hot day, the breeze on a shaded cart is welcome — even when passing by the sheep and swine barn.

If, like me, you can't resist baby animals, there are a few stops worth making. The fowl and rabbit barn has a hatch of holdable baby chicks that will peep their way into your heart.

There is also a baby calf on raffle outside the dairy barn.

On a tight budget it might seem hard to satisfy the appetite, but a goldmine of quality food at comparatively cheap prices can be found at the Grange food booth. Four hot dogs, two pieces of corn on the cob, two iced teas, and two tomato servings cost $10.

Another way to enjoy the fair at lower cost is to watch for special deal days. Some days of the week there are unlimited amusement ride passes for a fraction of the cost.

Individual tickets are otherwise $1 each, with the average ride taking three tickets.

After a long day at the fair, one looks for a relaxing finish. Every night the fair has a parade go through with bands, puppets and free candy flung into the crowd for those unafraid to dive for a Dum Dum Lollipop.

And, after arriving home, if you want to relive your fair adventure, just try smelling your map. Mine still smells like what the horses were eating on Sunday.

EPILOGUE

It's done; we won. The Third Infantry Division has left the fields of battle, victorious of course, and passed the torch on to the Fourth Infantry and many other units I am not familiar with. We defeated Saddam's ruffians at every turn, taking few casualties of our own, and raced to Baghdad faster than even the most hopeful forecast allowed.

Now that we have served our time and waited patiently in line for transportation, it is our due reward to return home to our lives.

I suppose this is really what we were fighting for the whole time. The regular soldiers were getting only a little news before, after, and during the conflict. We didn't care about Bush's campaign to gain international favor against Iraq. We didn't care about French and German wheedling, or even, really, about Saddam's cruelty. We wanted to go home.

If the shortest way home meant cutting a swath through the heart of Iraq, we were the right ones for the job. This is not to say that the reconstruction isn't vital, or that liberating a horribly oppressed people isn't a beautiful thing. It is. But these are not things that a person on his own can fight for. The ideas are too big, the concepts too vague when there are real live bullets being tossed around and your next objective is through them. We fought to live and return to our families.

What is it that Gandalf said? "It is no mean thing to live a quiet and simple life?" This is true. A hero's welcome is nice, but it lasts only for a moment. Great deeds are done and forgotten. What mattered to me was simply *a* welcome — back to my family and my friends and a return to normal life. We ventured forth into Mordor, not because we wanted to own it for ourselves, but so we could come back to our shire and see it untainted by evil.

I have this incredible desire to do the un-incredible things of life — to eat food from restaurants and sandwiches from my refrigerator, to make a phone call at my own leisure, and to spend perfect quiet moments with my wonderful girlfriend.

This is what we all fought for and what we all learned: the spoils of war are not picked up from the battlefield, they're waiting for you inside your house. My journey is complete. I see that God has taught me much and forced me to grow much, but, most of all, He has put my foot on the path to the next journey, the long one that we call living.

Dover, Delaware
August, 2003

JB'S GLOSSARY

113 — Armored personnel carrier.

577 — Similar to a 113 but with a higher top. They are often used as command vehicles and tend to have computers and electronics inside.

$^1/_{15}$ INF Coin — A coin from $^1/_{15}$ Infantry. An "attaboy."

AAM — Army Achievement Medal.

ACE — Armored bulldozer.

AFB — Air Force base.

AHA — Ammunition holding area.

AIT — Advanced infantry training.

APC — Armored personnel carrier.

APO — Army post office.

ARCOM — Army Commendation Medal.

ASVAB — This is the test you take to see if you're smart enough to be in the army. It has extremely low standards...

AT4 — launcher — A single-use bazooka.

BCT — Basic combat training.

BDE — Brigade.

BFST — A Bradley with some artillery-related equipment in it.

BII — Basic initial issue. This is all the garbage that comes with the Bradley, like shovels and water cans.

Bn Coin — See $^1/_{15}$ INF Coin. Bn is short for battalion.

Bravo 13 — One of the Bradleys I drove. The track naming system is simple: Company first, then platoon number, followed by an 1-4.

Class A — Dress uniform.

coax — The coaxially mounted machine gun. It shoots bullets rather than the much larger AP rounds of the main gun.

CQ — Charge of quarters. This is where you don't get to sleep for 24 hours in case the phone rings at three in the morning.

CRTT — I made this one up.

DI — Drill instructor. Same as a drill sergeant.

dismounts — Soldiers who are not drivers.

DNS — These are the military phones that connect all military posts around the world. With the help of an operator your call can be jumped from a DNS phone to a regular civilian line. This is how I called home, thanks to the wonderful and helpful people at Dover Air Force Base.

Dragon — A single-use bazooka with a guided missile.

EIB — Expert Infantryman's Badge.

FO — Forward observer for artillery.

FTX — Field training exercise.

HETs — Heavy equipment trucks.

Hind-V — A Russian combat helicopter.

HMMWVs — Humvee.

kabal — The place with the dirt wall around it where we lived. It is basically an assembly area in the middle of the desert. It has dirt walls about 10 feet high, guard towers, and a main gate with concrete barriers and guard posts.

Klicks – Kilometers.

Jarheads — Army word for Marines.

LNTT – I made this one up.

Miles — Multiple integrated laser engagement system. Laser tag with a budget.

MOS — Military occupational speciality.

MWR facilities — Morale, welfare, and recreation facilities.

NCO — Noncommissioned officer. A sergeant.

OCS — Officer candidate school.

PLL — Petroleum, liquids, and lubricants.

PLUT — I made this one up.

PMCS — Preventative maintenance checks and service.

pogues — Pogues are anyone who are not combat arms if you are talking to someone in combat arms, and they are anyone who is not infantry if you ask the infantry. It means anyone who is doing less work than you at any given time.

power take-off unit — Part of the Bradley that does, apparently, something important, because when mine broke the Bradley stopped working.

PX — Post exchange. It's the shops.

ratelo — Radio telephone operator.

RIP — Ranger indoctrination program. This is where people with weak minds and strong bodies wind up.

RPG – Rocket-propelled grenade.

SAW — Squad automatic weapon. A light machine gun.

SKO — I made this one up.

SP — Start point. Means either time or location. Some people make it a verb, as in, "We're going to SP from such and such a place."

Sta-Brite — Shiny medals and decorations for the Class A uniform.

T-80 — A Russian main battle tank.

TC — Track commander.

TOC — Tactical operations center.

TOW missile — Tubular-launch, optically tracked, wire-guided missile. A guided missile for the Bradley.

Turtles — Army word for Marines.

APPENDIX A

Death Comes to Nathan D. Alynnwood

Sickness has laid claim to Nathan's life. Death comes merely to serve the warrant. It pleases him to ride on a ghostly white stallion through the world of man. Pale horse and rider appear on the street in front of the house, illuminated by orange streetlamp and white starlight.

Death is not a murderer; Death is a force, a dispenser of consequences, the consequences of Man's twisted plans, Sickness's impersonal slaughter, and Happenstance's blindness. Over the course of the centuries Death has developed a sort of personality; he has begun to identify with his work, if not with his individual subjects. Tonight he has come to reap the life of one Nathan Darryl Alynnwood.

Death walks slowly and surely toward the last of tonight's appointments. His cowl billows in the chilly night breeze and his scythe glints briefly in the moonlight. His hood opens into an infinite void. No light penetrates into Death's visage; his expressions are as ineffable as the will that guides his hand.

Death has no need for doors or windows — he is as immaterial as a thought. He comes and goes according to his own silent needs and wishes, but tonight seems strange to him. As he walks up the wild unkempt yard, he sees Sickness slithering out of the house. Sickness is as immaterial as Death and he moves right through the front wall and into the lawn without a second thought. He sees Death and stops.

"It'sss about time you sssshowed." Sickness cocks his serpentine head to examine Death with one conniving eye.

"I come at the right time. And no sooner."

"He'ssss been ready for dayssss. Sssssome of usss think you are getting... ssssssoft..." Sickness lets a malignant grimace cross his features.

"When you are able to fulfill my duties, you may have them." With this, Death brushes past him toward the house. Sickness has already faded off into the night.

When Death reaches the front wall, he pauses. Immediately opposite of where he stands is the bedroom, where the form of Nathan D. Alynnwood lay somnolent. Any other night Death would have stepped through and with a grand arc of his scythe severed Nathan's soul from his earthly form. Death makes to step through but stops himself. Something in the way Sickness has so callously disregarded this mortal's property, his world, his — Death paused before saying out loud, "his humanity" — strikes him as so reprehensible that he steps back.

Nathan is just a mortal like any other, but maybe mortal is not such a humble thing. Death decides to leave the man with some shred of honor on his last night and walks around to the front door. Death opens the door silently and shuts it equally soundlessly.

The house is a small, one-story affair, but it is home to four people. Nathan's family sleeps also. The front door opens into a small foyer. Pictures of family outings on their boat hang from the walls. The center picture depicts Nathan holding up a Maui-Maui, and the fish is actually quite enormous. The kitchen is connected to the foyer, and a hallway heads to the bedrooms in one direction and to the living room in the other.

Death moves down the hallway toward Nathan's bedroom. At the terminus of the hallway, just outside of the master bedroom, Death sees a table pressed against the wall. The table is well worn, scratched, and buried underneath a stack of miscellaneous papers, pens, and a phone. A caller ID box is attached to the phone, and Death decides to scroll through the calls list. Judging from the last names — there are a few calls from family and several from friends or neighbors. There are also several calls from Grant Community Hospital, a local pharmacist, and a call from a Janssen and Wolff Holdings, Inc.

Death runs his skeletal hand across the pile of papers and then picks them up to better peruse them. Some are quick notes to various family members, reminder from mother to son about an assignment due in the morning, a reminder from son to mother to buy a certain brand of pudding for his school lunch. Nathan neither writes, nor is written to, in any of these.

There are also a few letters, most addressed to Janice Alynnwood. These were from immediate relatives and all of them expressed sorrow about Nathan's condition and contained perfunctory offerings of assistance. Some of them were worn around the edges from repeated reading.

To the side of the personal letters lay two envelopes from one Janssen and Wolff Holdings, Inc. The first was printed on a corporate letterhead and contained a form letter with their name slightly off-center in a bold font. Further down, the name of Grant Community Hospital was printed in the same slightly off-center boldface. The letter went on to explain that the account payable to the hospital, totaling $7,632.88, had been transferred to Janssen and Wolf, and a series of acceptable forms of payment were listed.

The second letter from Janssen and Wolff Holdings, Inc., collection agency lay unopened underneath the first. Death left it as it was.

"There is a story here," says Death to himself and he turns away from Nathan's bedroom, intent on uncovering more of it. Nathan's sons sleep in the bedroom next to their father's. Death turns the knob silently and lets himself in.

The oldest lays curled in the fetal position, clutching a worn baseball mitt. He is wearing pajamas and an Oakland A's baseball cap. He mumbles occasionally in his sleep and rolls over as Death watches him. Next to his bed is an open backpack, clearly not designed to hold the sheer quantity of papers and books stuffed into it.

Like all boys his age, every graded and returned assignment from the first day of school is haphazardly stuffed into the backpack, never to see the light of day again. Death shuffles through them and notes a marked decrease in the grades. He was making straight A's about four to six months ago, but since then he has dropped about a letter grade a month. Among the more recent papers is a series of teacher's notices sent home with increasing frequency to his parents. There is a space for the parents to initial upon receipt, and these are universally blank.

The boy had earned his first red F just yesterday. Stapled to the homework is a more seriously worded teacher's notice. The assignment and its attachment have been stuffed all the way down to the bottom of the backpack.

Next to the bed is a crib. On a small shelf next to it is a baby monitor. The red LED glows. The baby has a slight wheeze to his breathing, but otherwise sleeps soundly. Death looks at the baby's form for a long moment and then pulls the covers all the way up to the child's neck.

When the baby's own day comes, Death will be there waiting, but until then he will sleep soundly. In between the knife-edge of now and the final breath, there is an entire tapestry of life to be lived — a life that will grow and expand and connect with countless other lives but never hold any memories of the man who brought him into this world. The child will know his father only from the pictures he sees, like the ones hanging in the foyer.

Death ponders this for a minute and then walks out of the room and back to the foyer. He stares at the pictures again, this time seeing them from a new perspective. Before, they were merely frozen seconds in a man's life to help when memories failed, now Death sees them as the baby will, when he is older. These fragments are the windows through which the child will know the father; tiny and incomplete as they are, they are all he will have to form an image of his father.

Death steps back from the photographs and makes a right hand turn into the kitchen. Here, there is more evidence of the current state of the Alynnwood family's affairs. There are a few photographs on the counters. One is the family, less the baby, standing in a yard. The backdrop is a medium-sized, two-story brick house. The yard is in much better shape than this one. Death picks up the photo and looks at the back. The date is written in loose feminine cursive. Just over nine months ago. Six months ago their house was twice the size. There were two cars in the driveway; only one of them is still with them.

Janice smiles happily in the picture, one arm around her husband's waist, the other resting on her stomach. There is a slight bulge showing that she is early into her pregnancy. She rests her hands over her unborn baby with affection and protection.

A pad of stationery lay next to the phone. The letterhead said "Nathan Alynnwood, CPA" at the top and gave an address and several phone numbers at the bottom. He must have been self-employed. He probably had no insurance, or if he did, not nearly enough to cover the treatments for his cancer.

On the refrigerator were homework assignments with big red A's and a few colorings done by the oldest son. The son displayed the beginnings of a real artistic talent. One in particular stands out to Death.

It had the childish innocence of all the others, but the message must surely have stung. It depicted two houses side by side, obviously the former and the current. The current was dwarfed by the old, and in comparison the picture made the old house look almost palatial. They were labeled simply "Old House" and "New House."

From the kitchen, Death can see into the living room. The mother sleeps on the couch, face down with one hand hanging off the edge — the light still on and the radio burbling softly to itself. Next to it, the other half of the baby monitor system stands silent. Strewn around the couch is a filing cabinet's worth of paperwork.

Death kneels beside her and sifts through the mess, carefully though, so as to return everything as it was. There are a dozen incidental bills for small items and memberships long past due. Another collection agency was represented, their form letter states that they had taken over the account from Janssen and Wolff, Inc. and the current amount due is $8,777.81. Several identical letters from the same company, differing only in date, were stapled together.

In a separate pile were loan applications from a score of different agencies. Most were coupled with a rejection notice. Handwritten letters, some demanding, some stoic, and some shamelessly pleading were attached to all of these. A half-finished letter, the last of the batch, dangles limply from Janice's slender hand. She sleeps with a pen in her mouth; a small drool stain is beginning to form on the armrest.

Under her stomach lay an open day planner. Death could read the top half that protruded from her body. The date was tomorrow and it is filled with appointments: doctor, school, meetings with various financial companies and banks, and more that Death couldn't make out without pulling the book out from under her. He declines to do so, stands up and creeps out of the room.

On the way out he quietly flicks the table lamp off.

Death has seen enough to piece together the heart of the story. Reluctantly he returns to the hallway leading to Nathan's bedroom. He enters the bedroom and stares at Nathan's fitfully sleeping form with a mixture of pity and respect. Death raises his scythe like he has millions of times before, but this time slowly — hesitantly.

He looks around the room furtively, hoping for one last distraction. To his relief, and coupled with a pang of shame, one presents itself.

A leather-bound book, much larger than a novel or even a coffee table book, sits on a chair in the corner. Death lowers his scythe and picks up the book.

It is a scrapbook. The cover is burgundy leather and wordless. Each page is made of thick black cardstock with a clear laminate cover on both sides. This book is full of photographs, letters, and pictures. All of them are about Nathan.

Death starts at the first page, a clipping of Nathan's birth announcement in the local paper, and reads each entry carefully. The next page starts with a clipping about Nathan finishing first in a children's swim team at age six. He had participated in pinewood derby racing, campouts, and other scouting events, some mentioned in the newspaper, others captured in grainy color pictures.

Interspersed amongst the pages are handwritten commentaries in white ink. Some are as simple as, "I don't remember this," which referenced a story about Nathan calling an ambulance to an accident at age eight while adults stood shocked and immobile. Others are colorful commentaries on exactly what was going through his head at the time, some of them taking up entire pages.

Tickets to ball games, marked "Dad's ticket" and "my ticket" appear in the corners of some pages. There are a few brochures from plays and even one from the Baltimore Aquarium, obviously a significant moment, because it is circled three times.

As the pages turn the clippings become less yellowed and the color quality improves in the photos. There are more clippings about his altruistic deeds but also the nostalgic debris of his teen years — photos of bikes and cars he owned, parties with schoolmates, and some course syllabi from his high school and college classes. Notes fill the margins; some rather pointedly indicate how little he thought of certain teachers or their material.

There are pictures of his days of dating Janice (curiously no other women are featured, perhaps the book was put together after they were married or edited afterward). Tickets to concerts they shared and snippets of sappy love letters are arranged around pictures of the two of them. This section ends with their marriage announcement in the paper and a slew of wedding pictures.

Death notes that from this point on the handwritten notes are often in Janice's script. They alternate commenting on different events and sometimes both comment on major milestones in their lives. Sometimes they even comment on each other's previous comments. They must have worked simultaneously on this book.

Death pictures them curled up together drinking coffee, the huge scrapbook open across both of their laps while pasting in pictures and clippings and playfully fighting over who gets to write about what.

There are countless instances of Nathan's generosity. He donates money to charities. He gives his four employees at the accounting firm a day off in the middle of the week — provided they help him landscape the church grounds. He volunteers at hospitals. He raises money for so many causes that the comments are frequently short. "This one went well." "This one bombed." "I don't remember doing this one, but it says we raised a lot of money." An entire chapter is devoted to their adoption of a three-year-old Filipino boy. This must be the oldest son sleeping in the next room.

There are family trips to the zoo and colorings and homework assignments, all with high marks, mixed in with favorite recipes and a few baseball and hockey cards.

Another chapter is devoted to their newborn: Adam Hunter Alynnwood. The family is clearly enamored with their newest addition. There is one more clipping after that, a human-interest story about adults continuing their education. His name is mentioned. He had enrolled to take a drawing class and a history class. He never finished either because shortly afterward the symptoms of the cancer became too pronounced for him to carry on a normal life.

Here the notebook ends abruptly with seven blank pages left. Perhaps the Alynnwoods felt at this point that they had nothing nice at all to say and chose to say nothing at all.

Death closes the book, sits down on the chair, and places the book on his lap. He looks from its cover to its subject and back to its cover. So much life, recorded in short snippets, fills its pages full past overflowing, and yet somehow the living, breathing creator of all those moments seems hollow and empty as he lay sick in his bed.

Death stares at Nathan for a dozen long moments. He gathers his resolve. He is Death after all, and he has a job to perform. Conflicting thoughts churn in Death's mind.

It all seems so wrong to him. This man is needed by his wife, his family. He did great things with the time he was given; he would surely do many more great things if he had more time. No! This was not right at all, but neither was shirking his eternal duty. Who was he to decide who lived and who died? He merely served the warrant.

Death raises his scythe swiftly over his head, and ever so slowly, ever so softly lowers it back down and leans it up against the wall. He is Death, and he decides then — who better to choose who lives and dies than he?

Now that he had resolved not to send Nathan on to the afterlife, Death feels a sense of relief. It's as if all the strangeness of tonight has lifted from him and things are back to normal, no, better than before.

He still stares at Nathan — the man Nathan, the first mortal granted a second chance by Death. Nathan's life has been handed back to him from the very edge of eternity.

Nathan seems to sense a change too. He stirs in his sleep and his eyelids flutter open. For a half moment Death wonders if Nathan can see him. But, of course, he cannot, and Nathan's eyes wander listlessly around the room.

A faint moan escapes his lips and his eyes close again for so long that Death wonders if Nathan has returned to his slumber. But, he is still awake and his hand leaves the cocoon of blankets to feel around on the nightstand for pen and paper. Nathan writes a brief scrawl in a shaky, nearly illegible blur. Finished, he places the paper back on the stand. He tries to put the pen back on top of it, but his quivering hand misses the mark and the pen falls to the floor.

Death leans over, silently as always, to read what Nathan had scribbled. The writing is messy, so different from the bold hand that had marked the pages of the scrapbook. It appears that in his cancer-weakened state Nathan is unable to finish the note. Death reads aloud.

"Dearest Janice: I love you deeply, and I am deeply sorry. This pain — "

Death turns sharply around just in time to see Nathan fire a single shot from a .38 revolver into his own temple.

Stunned, Death begins, slowly at first, and then steadily growing louder, to weep.

APPENDIX B

Desert Tales

This appendix is a home for some of the wonderful stories I've picked up from other people I've encountered in the service. Some are from the Gulf War, others from our deployments to Iraq. There was really no place in the narrative for them, but I feel like they should be told.

Camel vs. Tank

This event was witnessed by one of my counterpart drivers while I was still in B Company during the first Kuwait rotation. He swears up and down it is true.

It was another hot Kuwait day and we were doing some cross training with our sister tank battalion. We were overwatching the tanks' movement across a large berm. [Author's Note: This means they were perched near the top of the berm so they could see across and were allowing the tanks to pass in front of them. This keeps them from barreling into an ambush or something. The tanks would then return the favor by overwatching for us on the next berm.]

We didn't see any enemy troops, so we let the tanks know it was clear to move. Boy can they move too! Tanks are incredibly fast, especially compared to our Bradleys. I've heard that without the turret on they can reach 100 mph, and the only reason they can't go faster is the tracks start to fly apart. With the turret on they can easily break 60 mph.

As the tanks reached the front end of the berm, I noticed that a lone camel had wandered into the path of the oncoming tanks. I suggested to the lieutenant that we call them and let them know, but he was confident that the driver would see the camel when they crested the berm.

He didn't take into account how fast the tanks were going. When the tanks crested the berm they practically leaped into the air! The driver couldn't see the camel until the front end of the tank came back down, and that was maybe seconds before — SPLAT! — the camel was roadkill.

The tank in question also happened to be equipped with a mine plow, which is referred to as the Tiger Claw, for visually appropriate reasons.

Well, after the tanks continued on their way, we just *had* to take a look at the ex-camel. Here's the creepy part: We found nothing more than some loose hair! We figure either the tanks slammed into it so hard it actually drove the camel under the sand, or (my personal favorite explanation) the impact utterly vaporized the camel. To this day I wish I knew exactly which tank that was so I could quiz the driver about what he saw.

Camel vs. Injector

This is a story told to me by one of our old squad leaders back in B Co. It took place during the Gulf War.

So they give us these kits in case we ever get slimed by some kind of chemical or biological agent. It's two shots together in a little case. Being the curious kind of guy that I am, I ask what's in it. They tell me it's called atropine, and I ask them what exactly it's going to do to my body when I inject myself. Of course, he doesn't exactly know.

I decide I'm going to find out before I, or any of my men, go squirting it into our bloodstream. To my great fortune a herd of camels happens to be in the vicinity. I grab another troop to be the distractor and we move up to one that's kind of separated from the herd. My partner gets the animal's attention with a bit of his MRE and slowly feeds it to him. I move around to the backside, just oblique of the kicking area, and prepare my needle.

I figure I'm only gonna get one shot at this so I decide to hit him with both needles at once, it's not as scientific, but hey. I clutch both needles in my hand, rear back, and BLAM! I sock it to him! The camel jumps forward and runs about 50 meters away, but then he stops and goes back to grazing. I guess if you're that big a couple of needles is about equal to a mosquito to us.

My assistant says, "Well, I guess they're safe, huh Sarge?"

"You don't know that yet," I reply.

*"Righto mates, what we have here is a camel. Let's see what happens
when we shoot him up with a little dose of — HOLY COW!"*

We watch patiently for about a minute, then the camel lets out
a big sigh and proceeds to fall over sideways. We ran over to
check it out, and it was stone dead. Those two little shots killed
a 500-pound animal in less than five minutes.

My partner in crime looks at me with wide eyes and says,
"Why do they give us *three* kits, Sarge?"

"I don't know; I just don't know."

[Author's note: I described this event to a pharmacist friend
of the family and he explained that atropine influences your
metabolism and heart rate in an attempt to clear out any chemical or biological agent. But without the negative effects of these

"I told you already – NO pork!"

agents for it to counterbalance, it'll kill you thoroughly. He told me that of course it would kill a perfectly fine camel, but if that camel had been contaminated it could have saved it. Still, I may take my chances with the anthrax...]

The MRE Thief

I once spent a week guarding our food preparation facility in Kuwait. This was a few days of pulling shifts by the bunker at the entrance of the facility. The squad we relieved told us about a particular nomad who would pass back and forth by the facility.

This nomad had a little dog that he would send in to steal food. The dog was small enough to slip under the wire, fast enough that you didn't have a prayer of catching him, and smart enough to grab an MRE out of an open box and rush back out of the wire with it. A few minutes later we'd see the nomad happily snacking on whatever culinary delights had been returned to him. He'd give us a little smug wave, and we'd have to grudgingly admire his system.

However, one time when the little dog brought him a meal, he started yelling at the dog and then threw it at him. We couldn't figure out what was wrong until we looked to see what was missing: pork chow mein, one of the few pork MREs in the box and one that his Muslim beliefs wouldn't allow him to eat!

FROM BASIC TO BAGHDAD

is available online or through your favorite bookstore or home-school supplier. Quantity discounts are available to qualifying institutions.

All Bright Ideas Press books are available to the booktrade and educators through all major wholesalers.

For more information on *From Basic to Baghdad*, visit:

www.FromBasictoBaghdad.com

Brave Ideas is a publishing imprint of Bright Ideas Press. Bright Ideas Press specializes in publishing quality educational curricula. For more information, visit:

www.BrightIdeasPress.com

BRAVE
IDEAS